2 4 JAN 2018

D0586810

Please return this book on or before the date shown above. To
renew go to www.essex.gov.uk/libraries, ring 0845 603 7628 or
go to any Essex library.

Essex County Council

BABY
NAMES
2014

Ella Joynes

white
LADDER

Acknowledgements

I would like to extend my utmost gratitude to Cerys Owen, Shelley Heck, Michael Turner and Robin Boothroyd for their contributions; without them this book would have been much shorter. My thanks are also given to Beth Bishop, Libby Walden and Jessica Spencer at Crimson Publishing for their patience and guidance throughout the project. Finally, the greatest thanks go to my children, Owen Henri and Jasper Hugh. I fall more in love with them and their names, every day.

This fourth edition published in Great Britain 2013 by
Crimson Publishing Ltd
The Tramshed, Walcott Street, Bath BA1 5BB

First, second, third and fourth editions published by Crimson Publishing in 2009, 2010, 2011 and 2012.

© Crimson Publishing, 2013

A catalogue record for this book is available from the British Library.

ISBN 978 1 908281 57 9

Typeset by IDSUK (DataConnection) Ltd
Printed and bound by L.E.G.O. S.p.A, Lavis TN

Contents

Introduction   1

PART ONE   3

1. What was hot in 2013?   5
2. What does 2014 hold for baby names?   23
3. How to choose a name   33
4. Registering a baby's name   65
5. Naming twins, triplets, and more   71

PART TWO Boys' Names A–Z   77

PART THREE Girls' Names A–Z   217

A note on how to use this book

While the author and publisher acknowledge that baby names vary widely in spelling and pronunciation, this book lists each name only once: under the most common initial and spelling. If a name has an alternative spelling with a different initial, it may be listed under that letter also.

Information relating to statistics and trends in baby names is based on the most recent data at the time of writing.

Introduction

As daunting as it might sound at first, choosing a name for your baby is one of the most enjoyable decisions you get to make as a new parent.

However, baby-naming is not without its pitfalls. Sometimes choosing the right name is simply a case of hearing one you like and knowing instantly that it's the one. Then again, for some parents the naming game gets far more complicated when they start trying to please parents, grandparents, friends and siblings, while trying to avoid names that could be shortened into ridiculous nicknames or would make for funny initials.

And here's another thing: you'll probably want to choose something unique – but not too unique – or something common – but not too common. A name could be inspired by a celebrity you admire, a sports star, or an influential historical or royal figure. It could also come from the family tree or follow a current baby-naming trend. And don't forget that you need to make sure that you love it – you and your baby will have to live with it forever! The possibilities are endless so it's understandable that it can throw some parents into panic mode.

Well, never fear: *Baby Names 2014* is here to take you through your options and solve your baby-naming dilemmas. It's updated annually, so it always includes the year's most popular names, those that are making a comeback and celebrity choices. We've included dozens of lists to provide you with inspiration and, of course, couldn't resist looking at some downright weird names that children have been given over the years (usually by celebs).

Take a peek at the most up-to-date trends in baby-naming: from the backlash against quirky names to the return of the traditional, headed up, of course, by Prince George. Read about how movie stars and the characters they play influence how we name our children, what teachers really think about the names in their classrooms and what happened to baby-naming trends when a new Pope was elected in 2013.

Be sure to keep an eye out for all the facts and figures we have got for you – including what names are most popular – so that you can either go with the flow . . . or deliberately against it.

This book is broken into two sections: the first deals with choosing your baby's name through a series of questions and suggestions and the second gives you a meaning for each name you are considering. There's no right or wrong way to use this book, just as there's no right or wrong way to make your baby-naming decision.

Remember: picking a name should be fun! Grab a pencil, dip in and find some names you like. Use the tons of suggestions we've given you to work out if one of them is your baby's new name.

Good luck!

part one

1

What was hot in 2013?

When Harry met Amelia . . .

Last year, the most popular name for baby boys in England and Wales was Harry, which isn't that surprising given its recent appearance all over modern literature (Harry Potter), pop culture (Harry Styles, from One Direction) and our affection for the Royal Family (Prince Harry). It knocked Oliver off pole position and also managed to keep the name Jack from climbing back up after its 16-year spell at number one. However, the name Jack hasn't moved from the top spot since 2003 in Northern Ireland and it has also reigned supreme in Scotland for the last five years. Harry does appear in the Top 10 lists in both countries, though (in fourth place in Northern Ireland and in eighth position in Scotland), which means that, throughout the UK, Harry is number one.

The most popular name for baby girls in England and Wales was Amelia. Interestingly, it pushed Olivia off the top spot by jumping up a whopping four places – an impressive feat when you're discussing the Top 10.

Top 10 baby names

Boys	Girls
1. Harry	1. Amelia
2. Oliver	2. Olivia
3. Jack	3. Lily
4. Alfie	4. Jessica
5. Charlie	5. Emily
6. Thomas	6. Sophie
7. Jacob	7. Ruby
8. James	8. Grace
9. Joshua	9. Ava
10. William	10. Isabella

Among the girls' names, there were two new entries to the Top 10 last year: Ava (ninth) and Isabella (10th). The latter, which means 'pledged to God' in Spanish, has not strayed far from the Top 10 since the original release of the Twilight books and films in 2005, while Ava has slowly been increasing in popularity over the last 12 years – an astonishing jump from position 196 in 2001 to ninth last year. There was less of a change to the line-up in boys' names, with the only new entry being Jacob, in seventh place. Again, the surge in popularity for Jacob can, in part, be attributed to Stephenie Meyer's Twilight series.

Other new entries to the Top 100 for boys include: Tommy, Blake, Frankie, Elijah and Jackson. The boys' names that dropped off the Top 100 to make room for these newcomers are: Aidan, Bradley, Brandon, Kieran and Sam.

By George!

The most anticipated baby of 2013 was, of course, the royal baby. After his birth on 22 July 2013, the Duke and Duchess of Cambridge revealed they had chosen the names George Alexander Louis for our future king. Will and Kate did not part with tradition, and chose names of past monarchs and names with strong family ties. There have been six British monarchs called George, including the Queen's father, George VI (although his first name was actually Albert and he was known as Bertie). George is also one of Prince Charles' middle names. Alexander is said to have been a favourite of Kate's and is also the Duke of Edinburgh's grandfather's middle name. Alexandra is also one of the Queen's middle names. The choice of Louis was not a surprise – it is one of both William's and his father Charles' middle names. They were both named in honour of Lord Louis Mountbatten, the Duke of Edinburgh's uncle.

For the girls' Top 100 there were several newcomers: Bella, Willow, Elsie, Kayla, Francesca and Lydia. The names that left the Top 100 were: Aimee, Alexandra, Laila, Libby, Maisy and Tilly.

So, what baby name trends were popular last year?

Names going up the Top 100

Boys	**Girls**
Arthur	Eliza
Dexter	Evelyn
Jensen	Harriet
Riley	Sofia

Names going down the Top 100

Boys	**Girls**
Ben	Caitlin
Cameron	Katie
Kyle	Keira
Lewis	Lauren
Reece	Tia

66 All British people have plain names, and that works pretty well over there. 99

Paris Hilton

Being creative with tradition

Last year, the Office for National Statistics (ONS) reported that the Top 10 names for both boys and girls represented only 14% of all live births in the country. This means that a whopping 86% of names chosen by parents in 2013 were so diverse in spelling that they did not land in the most popular group, as the ONS counts each spelling as a separate entry. For example, if one child is named Lily (ranked third) and another is called Lilly (ranked 27th), they are still counted separately from their nursery-mates Lillie (112th) and Lili (458th). Hyphenated names are also separated: Lily-Mae, Lily-May and Lily-Mai are all counted as individual names in the UK's official statistics.

Some of Britain's quirky baby names during the last year have included: Bunny, Gift, Ha, Lwsi and Ziqra for a girl, and Arry, Great, Luv, Rock and Zvi for a boy.

Compare this to 50 years ago, when nearly 50% of all names appeared in the Top 25, and you'll see why this is so surprising.

Traditional names still dominate the charts: the Top 10 for both boys and girls has been made up of pretty much the same names for the last 10 years. However, now we are seeing a trend where parents pick a traditional name and change the spelling. Take a fairly conservative name like Holly. It ranked 18th 10 years ago but it's since fallen to 26th place. Hollie, however, has moved up a couple of places in that time (possibly due to the birth of Amanda Holden's daughter: Hollie Rose) and Holli, which is a fairly unusual spelling of this name, was given to exactly 10 babies last year – the first year it's appeared. Also appearing were the variations: Holleigh, Lollie, Halle and Hallie.

Top 10 baby names in Scotland

Boys	Girls
1. Jack	1. Sophie
2. Lewis	2. Emily
3. Riley	3. Olivia
4. James	4. Ava
5. Logan	5. Lucy
6. Daniel	6. Isla
7. Ethan	7. Lily
8. Harry	8. Jessica
9. Alexander	9. Amelia
10. Oliver	10. Mia

Although names such as Alfie, Archie, Harry, Lily and Harriet had dropped out of mainstream use by the 1970s and become vastly unpopular, in the last few years names ending in -a, -ie and -y have started to see a resurgence, particularly as a spelling option for parents who like the sound of a traditional name but want to give it a modern twist. Other old-fashioned names, such as Arthur, Ava, Florence and Sebastian, have climbed the popularity ranks in the Top 100 lists, joining such stalwarts as Alexander, Alice, Grace and Thomas.

The traditional Muslim name Mohammed has now become so popular in the UK that if just the three spelling variations in the Top 100 were counted as the same name, it would be the third most popular name for baby boys in the country. The spelling 'Mohammed' is the most common (ranked 19th), followed by 'Muhammad' (22nd) and 'Mohammad' (63rd).

Top 10 baby names in Northern Ireland

Boys	Girls
1. Jack	1. Sophie
2. James	2. Grace
3. Matthew	3. Emily
4. Ethan	4. Sophia
5. Daniel	5. Lily
6. Harry	6. Chloe
7. Ryan	7. Lucy
8. Charlie	8. Jessica
9. Conor	9. Olivia
10. Adam	10. Eva

66 Each generation wants new symbols, new people, new names. They want to divorce themselves from their predecessors. 99

Jim Morrison

Rising stars

Boys	Girls
Arthur	Bella
Blake	Eliza
Frankie	Elsie
Jensen	Harriet
Riley	Kayla
Sebastian	Rose
Tommy	Willow

Giving a baby boy a shortened version of a traditional name as his complete first name is becoming increasingly popular. Take the most popular boy's name, Harry, as an example. This in itself is a shortened version of Henry (28th) or Harold (1,158th), but it also lends itself – perhaps a little uneasily – to Harree (2,039th) or Arry (appearing on the charts for the first time last year in 4,647th place). The name James is never far from the Top 10, and last year its nickname Jamie slotted in at position 49. This has also happened with William (ranked 10th): Billy is 106th, Will is 269th and Wil appears further down. Surprisingly, though, the names 'Willy' and 'Willie' weren't given to a single child last year in the entire UK! I wonder why . . .

Lots of parents are now designing their own spellings and variations: last year there were 4,647 unique baby boy names and a whopping 5,785 baby girl names – which is nearly 100 more than the year before. This means that there are 10,432 completely unique names out there and some incredibly creative parents!

How about a name without vowels? Last year the names Cyd, KC, MD, My and Thy were all given to at least three children apiece.

And how do you spell that?

A selection of last year's original spellings for girls include: Caitie (from Katy), Tiffanie (from Tiffany), Lejla (from Leila), and Zoi, Zoie, Zoey and Zoeya (from Zoe). The spelling of Emily as Emeli can also be attributed to the stonking success of songstress Emeli Sandé. Boys' names variations include: Xzaviar (from Xavier), Juels (from Jules), Fynlee (from Finlay), and Rilee, Rileigh, Ryle, Rylea and Rylei (from Riley).

Heavenly hyphenation

One of the most common way parents use to add a twist to tradition is by hyphenating their children's names. There are over 1,000 names with a hyphen tacked on to the end of another name in this year's list.

Popular hyphens include: -Rose, -May/-Mae and -Leigh/ -Lee, which make names such as Lily-Rose, Ella-Rose, Gracie-Mae, Demi-Leigh and Lacey-May. If you add all the spelling variations together, names that end in May or Mae would be in the Top 20 and those that include Rose would be around position 50!

Boys are not exempt from this rule either, as it is becoming fashionable to add -James or -Lee to the end of a baby boy's name. The highest-ranking version is Tyler-James (in position 510), with over 70 birth certificates to show for it. Also popular are Tommy-Lee, Alfie-James and Jayden-Lee.

Top 10 names in Australia

Boys	Girls
1. William	1. Ruby
2. Lucas	2. Charlotte
3. Oliver	3. Emily
4. Noah	4. Olivia
5. Jack	5. Chloe
6. Ethan	6. Amelia
7. Thomas	7. Mia
8. Lachlan	8. Sophie
9. Joshua	9. Isabella
10. James	10. Ava

The cult of celebrity

Celebrities are infamous for choosing obscure names for their babies, but last year's birth announcements seemed to be a little more conservative than usual with the royals leading the way. The Duke and Duchess of Cambridge chose the traditional name George for their son.

Recent deliveries from the celebrity stork have included some really traditional baby girl names: Theodora (Robbie Williams), Margot (Sophie Dahl) and Marnie Rose (Lily Allen). The same has happened for boys: Angelo (Adele), Alfred (David Walliams), Noah (Megan Fox) and Felix (Hugh Grant). There were a sprinkling of weird ones too, though (Rocky and Spike spring to mind, thanks to Sarah Michelle Gellar and Edith Bowman . . .), but then a list of celebrity baby names wouldn't be without them! Unsurprisingly, given her rather alternative name, Peaches (Honeyblossom) Geldof, who chose a quirky name for her first son (Astala Dylan Willow), named her new son Phaedra (actually a female name in Greek mythology) Bloom Forever.

Royalty revealed

Fortunately, Will and Kate didn't keep us waiting long to unveil their choice of baby name. The name Prince George Alexander Louis was announced just two days after his birth. This is quick by royal standards – the Palace took a week to reveal Prince William's name in 1982 and nearly a month to unveil Prince Charles' in 1948. Some were surprised at the restraint the couple showed in choosing only three names – both William and Charles have four names, and the Queen's uncle Edward VIII had seven!

In the latest lists issues by the ONS, George is the 12th most popular name, Alexander is at number 23 and Louis at number 68. It will be interesting to see how high these three names climb up the charts this year. We are betting on at least the top 10! The little prince will be officially known as His Royal Highness Prince George of Cambridge.

There's a bit of a trend among celebrity parents at the moment for choosing names of cities or other geographical features, such as Camden (chosen by both Nick Lachey and Kristen Cavallari for their sons), Milan (Shakira's baby boy) and Tennessee (Reece Witherspoon's new baby boy). Of course, this is hardly a new trend: the Beckhams were notorious for choosing the name Brooklyn for their son in 1999, after announcing that he was conceived in the New York City suburb. Other recent place names include Moroccan (Mariah Carey's son), Adalaide (Katherine Heigl's adopted daughter) and Penelope Scotland (Kourtney Kardashian's second child).

Celebrity babies of 2013

Angelo James (Adele and Simon Konecki)

Penelope Scotland (Kourtney Kardashian and Scott Disick)

Olive (Drew Barrymore and Will Kopelman)

Noah Shannon (Megan Fox and Brian Austin Green)

Cyrus Michael Christopher (Claire Danes and Hugh Dancy)

Rocky James (Sarah Michelle Gellar and Freddie Prinze Jr.)

Theodora Rose (Robbie Williams and Ayda Field)

Felix Chang (Hugh Grant and Tinglan Hong)

Milan (Shakira and Gerard Piqué)

Rainbow Aurora (Holly Madison and Pasquale Rotella)

Margot (Sophie Dahl and Jamie Callum)

Tennessee James (Reece Witherspoon and Jim Toth)

Rex Rayne (Fearne Cotton and Jesse Wood)

Marnie Rose (Lily Allen and Sam Cooper)

Spike (Edith Bowman and Tom Smith)

Lulu Rosylea (Bryan Adams and Alicia Grimaldi)

Fox India (Mark Owen and Emma Ferguson)

Florence Aurelia Alice (Jake and Harriet Humphrey)

Phaedra (Peaches Geldof and Thomas Cohen)

Klay Anthony Alfred (Coleen and Wayne Rooney)

Alfred (David Walliams and Lara Stone)

Everly (Channing Tatum and Jenna Dewan-Tatum)

Alaia-May (Rochelle and Marvin Humes)

North (Kim Kardashian and Kanye West)

Ace (Jessica Simpson and Eric Johnson)

Prince George Alexander Louis (The Duke and
    Duchess of Cambridge)

Baby girl (Penelope Cruz and Javier Bardem)

Wacky celebrity baby names of recent years

Bingham Hawn (Kate Hudson and Matthew
    Bellamy, also parents to Ryder)

Blue Ivy (Beyoncé Knowles and Jay Z)

Buddy Bear Maurice (Jules and Jamie Oliver, also
    parents to Poppy Honey, Daisy Boo and Petal
    Blossom Rainbow)

Cosima Violet (Claudia Schiffer and Matthew
    Vaughn, also parents to Caspar and Clementine)

Ever Imre (Alanis Morissette and Mario Treadway)

Harper Seven (Victoria and David Beckham, also
    parents to Brooklyn, Romeo and Cruz)

Holiday Grace (Harold and Brittany Perrineau)

Ikhyd (M.I.A. and Ben Brewer)

Kahekili Kali (Evangeline Lilly and Norman Kali)

Rainbow Aurora (Holly Madison and Pasquale Rotella)

Rosalind Arusha Arkadina Altaluna Florence (Uma Thurman and Arpad Busson)

Spike (Edith Bowman and Tom Smith)

Astala Dylan Willow (Peaches Geldof and Thomas Cohen; also parents to Phaedra)

Pop culture

The impact of characters in TV programmes, movies, and books has been huge on baby names in the last few years. In 2013 the film *The Great Gatsby* piqued our interest in names from a bygone era: the 1920s. Jay, Daisy, Nick, Myrtle and Tom were starting to become fairly common names during this decade, but many of them became deeply unfashionable within 40–50 years. However, names have ways of coming back around after enough time has passed, and this is certainly true for names from that era. For example, the name 'Jay' doesn't appear anywhere in the Top 100 names for boys during the 1920s, but 'James', which Jay is short for, reached fourth place in 1924. Although by 1964 it had sunk to 19th place, by 1984 it was in second place again. This pattern is repeated often: Daisy (the 88th most popular name for baby girls in 1924) doesn't appear anywhere on the Top 100 by 1974 but last year it was right back up again, in position 20. This trend is definitely set to continue, so who knows? Maybe Myrtle will make a comeback! (Probably not, though: only four babies were given that name in 2013 . . .)

Other movies, however, didn't seem to inspire parents as much. *Star Trek Into Darkness* and *The Hobbit: The Desolation of Smaug* were both massive box office hits but parents didn't seem as keen to choose the characters' names for their babies as usual. It's extremely likely that in these two instances the names are just too 'out there' for most of us; for example, only 12 families chose to name their babies Kirk (after Captain Kirk) and as for Bilbo Baggins . . . well . . .

The movie trilogy based on The Hunger Games novels provided parents with a whole host of alternative spellings for already popular names. Last year the second film, *Catching Fire*, came out, although it was too late in the year to affect baby names significantly. However, since the books and original movie were released, the names Peeta and Gale have entered the boys' names lists for the first time ever, and it's only a matter of time before Katniss herself becomes an influence on girls' names. The name Primrose, or 'Prim', has started to climb the charts, confirming the idea that parents are starting to choose old-fashioned names again.

Other influential books include the runaway success of *Fifty Shades of Grey*, which is rumoured to be released as a film sometime in 2014. The main characters, Anastasia (Ana) and Christian, persuaded many parents to use their names for their babies. Anastasia has jumped from 383rd place to a position in the Top 200, while Christian, which was in 204th place a few years ago, is set to be in the Top 100 next year.

Did you know that the Queen gets a say in what new princes and princesses are called? In 1988, Princess Beatrice was going to be called Annabel but the Queen dismissed it as 'too yuppie', according to the *Sun* newspaper. She suggested the more traditional Beatrice and it stuck. Maybe she had the final say in Prince George's naming – George was her father's name, after all!

Television shows are definitely a source of inspiration for new parents, as demonstrated by the latest series of *Downton Abbey*, which has continued to impress parents. The name Violet, for example (from Maggie Smith's acerbic character Violet Crawley, the Dowager Countess of Grantham), has proved the most popular: over 500 baby girls were given the name Violet last year.

An Israeli couple called their baby girl 'Like' after the Facebook button. Their other children are called Pie and Vash, which means honey.

Banned names around the world

@ – China
Chow Tow (meaning 'smelly head') – Malaysia
Mona Lisa – Portugal
Monkey – Denmark
Osama Bin Laden – Germany
0 – Sweden
Stompy – Germany

2

What does 2014 hold for baby names?

Will these trends continue?

Looking ahead to 2014, the trend for choosing a traditional name and altering the spelling looks set to continue. The 100-year rule also doesn't seem to be failing and names that were on the 1914 charts will likely appear in 2014.

For girls, soft-ending names will continue to dominate the charts. Half of the names in the Top 20 end in -a at the moment (including Amelia, Jessica, Ava, Isabella, Isla, Ella and Sophia), and names ending in -y or -ie sounds will also stick around for a few more years (think Lily, Emily, Sophie, Ruby, Evie and Chloe).

In the case of boys' names, trends are a little harder to pinpoint. There is also a great deal more shuffling in the ranks going on in the list of boys' names, with huge differences over the last 10 years. Therefore, it's probable that parents expecting baby boys in 2014 will be following trends such as nicknames and short names, instead of sound trends. This phenomenon can be seen emerging as Bobby becomes more popular than Robert (which dropped 50 places) and Alfie more popular than Alfred (sitting in fourth place, miles ahead of Alfred's 158th position).

Predicted Top 10 baby names in 2014

Boys	Girls
1. Harry	1. Amelia
2. Oliver	2. Olivia
3. Alfie	3. Ruby
4. Jack	4. Lily
5. George	5. Jessica
6. William	6. Grace
7. Jacob	7. Ava
8. Alexander	8. Sophie
9. Ethan	9. Emily
10. James	10. Isabella

2014 events

Other influences on the names that parents choose in 2014 may come from the worlds of sport, politics and celebrity.

In 2014 there are a couple of major sporting events and athletes who perform well at them will no doubt become inspirational for new parents. The Winter Olympics and Paralympics, hosted in Sochi, Russia, and the Commonwealth Games, hosted in Glasgow, Scotland, will be capitalising on the success of the 2012 London Olympics and Paralympics. The latter proved how inspirational great sporting stars could be and certainly influenced baby-naming decisions. Jessica Ennis (the gold medal-winning track and field athlete) saw her name move from sixth to fourth on the charts last year and another gold medallist, Mohamed 'Mo' Farah, might have been partially responsible for the continuing success of his name.

Also happening in 2014 is the FIFA World Cup, hosted in Brazil and the Women's World Cup. There is also the usual sprinkling of annual events, from Wimbledon's tennis to cycling's Tour de France. Bradley Wiggins, the cycling powerhouse, might have been the cause of the name Bradley jumping to position 105 last year after a spell of unpopularity in the early 2000s – and it's a name worth watching out for in 2014.

In terms of politics, 2014 is predicted to be a fairly quiet year, which will make a nice change. Politicians have a hazy history of influencing baby names; it's not true to say that children are frequently named after presidents or prime ministers, but there are exceptions. David Cameron's name keeps moving up and down the charts, with each year as unpredictable as the last: 'David' moved up seven places last year but was down the year before that, and overall it has dropped 11 spots in the last 10 years. His last name has appeared in the Top 100 pretty consistently over the last 30 years, though, and shows no sign of dropping out in the near future. President Barack Obama's name has yet to enter the Top 1,000 in the US and has never even been seen in UK statistics.

When Pope Francis I was elected last year, there was a flurry of parents choosing to honour him. The name Francis has now become a very popular choice for baby boys (and Frances for baby girls) in Catholic communities.

Interestingly, there is a trend of naming babies after the children of politicians; Barack Obama's daughters are named Maliyah and Sasha, and a variation of both of these appear in the US's Top 100 names for girls. When David Cameron's newborn daughter was named Florence in 2010, the media went wild and a flurry of parents started choosing this name for their baby girls shortly after. In fact, it jumped an astonishing 26 places the year when she was born, 11 in 2012, and has moved up 123 overall in the last 10 years.

Don't forget to register your baby's birth! Labour leader Ed Miliband came under scrutiny when he didn't register his first son's birth (Daniel) in 2009. As he and his partner, Justine Thornton, weren't then married, Miliband was supposed to attend the registration with her so that he could be listed as the baby's father but neglected to do so. He was present at the registration of his second son's birth (Samuel) in November 2010, though.

When former Prime Minister Margaret Thatcher died last year, there was speculation that such an iconic figure would influence baby-naming trends. Looking back, the name Margaret was at the height of its popularity during Thatcher's time as the country's leader, but it hasn't appeared in the Top 100 since the 1980s. In fact, last year it went down to position 557, with only 74 baby girls given that name. Its ranking doesn't seem to have been affected by her passing, though, as it's been around the same position for nearly 20 years. The name Maggie, however, is much more popular, landing at position 217 in last year's charts.

Britain's biggest baby was born last year, weighing 15lb at birth. His parents named him George and his the last name is King. King by name, king by nature!

2014 anniversaries

Significant anniversaries can potentially influence baby names – or at least provide parents with inspiration. In 2014 it will be the 450th anniversary of William Shakespeare's birth, 150 years since the birth of composer Richard Strauss and the 175th birthday of post-Impressionist artist Paul Cézanne.

Moreover, it will be 50 years since The Beatles were first introduced to the US and 30 years since the first Apple Macintosh computer went on sale; also, 20 years ago the Channel Tunnel was opened by Queen Elizabeth and French President François Mitterrand, and 15 years ago the Euro became an official currency.

Everybody do the dinosaur? Tahra Dactyl, who made the headlines because of her name, after being featured in a local newspaper article last year, must have parents with a sense of humour . . . or a serious interest in palaeontology.

In sporting history, it will be 90 years since the first Winter Olympics were held in Chamonix, France, and also the 60th anniversary of Roger Bannister running the four-minute mile.

Don't be surprised, therefore, if names linked to these anniversaries start becoming popular. As the media at large begins to broadcast these significant dates, names such as William (Shakespeare), Richard (Strauss and 'Ringo' Starr), Paul (Cézanne and McCartney), John (Lennon), George (Harrison), Apple (yes, really – think Gwyneth Paltrow's daughter), Elizabeth (Windsor), François (Mitterrand), Chamonix and Roger (Bannister) will start to be considered by parents as potential options for their baby names. And the more heavily they're promoted, the more frequently they'll be used.

2014 anniversary names

Boys	Girls
Benjamin	Apple
Charlie	Cézanne
Edward	Chamonix
George	Elizabeth

François	Frances
John	Georgina
Paul	Paula
Richard (Ringo)	Willa
Roger	
William	

The influence of pop culture

Pop culture will be perhaps the most prominent influence on baby names in the coming year. No doubt the names George, Alexander and Louis will skyrocket up the charts after Will and Kate's decision.

Celebrity couples expecting new arrivals include Frankie Sandford and Wayne Bridge, Halle Berry and Olivier Martinez, and Kate Winslet and Ned Rocknroll. If the choices of names these celebrities make are particularly noteworthy, they may well influence the choices made by the general population.

Beyoncé and Jay-Z have applied to trademark their daughter's name – not once, but twice. In 2013 the couple asked for 'Blue Ivy Carter' to be trademarked exclusively to them, for use with baby products and music.

Expected new arrivals in 2013

Jamie Bell and Evan Rachel Wood (Summer 2013)

Michael Bublé and Luisana Lopilato (Summer 2013 – boy)

Alec Baldwin and Hilaria Thomas (Summer 2013)

Fergie and Josh Duhamel (Summer 2013)

Lord Frederick Windsor and Sophie Winkleman (Summer 2013)

Lucy-Jo Hudson and Alan Halsall (Summer/Autumn 2013)

Sofia Vergara and Nick Loeb (Autumn 2013)

Halle Berry and Olivier Martinez (Autumn 2013)

Katie Price and Kieran Hayler (Autumn 2013)

Jake Buckley and Clair Meek (Autumn 2013 – boy)

Danielle and Jaime O'Hara (Autumn 2013)

Frankie Sandford and Wayne Bridge (Autumn 2013)

Caprice and Ty Comfort (Autumn 2013)

Ivanka Trump and Jared Kushner (Autumn 2013)

Jennifer Love Hewitt and Brian Hallisay (Winter 2013)

Kate Winslet and Ned Rocknroll (Winter 2013)

What's exciting about pop culture is how everything, from films and TV to books and blogs, can shape the world of baby names.

The year 2014 looks set to be the second year in a row of remakes, reboots and sequels. Upcoming movies in 2014 include yet another Wizard of Oz movie (an animation starring Lea Michele called *Legends of Oz: Dorothy's Return*), *Dumb and Dumber To* with Jim Carey and Jeff Daniels, *The Muppets . . . Again* (with, amongst others, Ricky Gervais and Tina Fey), and remakes of *Jumanji*, *The Flash*, *Robocop* and *Godzilla*. Examples of some new twists on old concepts are: *Maleficent*, starring Angelina Jolie and Elle Fanning, and a new Popeye film. There will also be several films based on books, such as *The Book Thief*, written originally by Markus Zusak.

2014 rising stars

Boys	Girls
Jeff (Jeffrey)	Angelina
Jim (James)	Aurora
Markus	Dorothy
Oz	Elle
Ricky	Liesel
Ryan	Tina

Remakes of old films are great for analysing how they have affected baby-naming over time. For example, when Walt Disney Studios released the original *Sleeping Beauty* cartoon in 1959, the name Aurora immediately moved up 80 places in the charts. In 2012 it appeared in the USA Top 200 for the first time and in position 404 in the UK, and after the new version – *Maleficent* – comes out in 2014, it may climb higher still. Another name to watch will be Liesel, which is the main character's name in *The Book Thief*. Liesel/Liesl became extremely popular in 1965, thanks to a member of the Von Trapp family in *The Sound of Music*, and it's possible that a successful film version of *The Book Thief* will have a similar impact in 2014.

Since the release of *Twilight* by Stephenie Meyer, Isabella and Jacob have surged up the charts. Even the surnames of these characters have increased in popularity: the name Cullen jumped 300 places in a single year.

Popular TV programmes set to air in 2014 include the third series of the popular *Call the Midwife* and the fourth series of the hit show *Downton Abbey*. There is also likely to be another *Doctor Who* series airing in 2014, as well as a potential new series of *Made in Chelsea*, and even a film being made of TOWIE (*The Only Way is Essex*)! So watch out for new baby names hitting the headlines, such as Trixie (*Call the Midwife*), Jane (*Call the Midwife*), Alfred (*Downton Abbey*), Ivy (*Downton Abbey*), Spencer (*Made in Chelsea*), Milly (*Made in Chelsea*), Gemma (*The Only Way is Essex*) and Mario (*The Only Way is Essex*). Maybe even Chummy (*Call the Midwife*) will make the charts next year!

3

How to choose a name

Top tips on choosing a name

- **Fall in love with the name(s) you've chosen.** If you plough through hundreds of names in this book and none of them jump off the page at you, then you probably haven't found the right one yet. Pick a name that makes you smile because if you love it, hopefully your child will too.

- **Don't listen to other people.** Sometimes, grandparents and friends will offer baby-naming 'advice', which may not always be welcome. If you've got your heart set on a name, keep it a secret until after the birth to avoid any unnecessary criticism. Trust your own instincts and remember: no one will really care once they see your baby. Its name will simply be its name.

A mother in Norway was jailed in 2007 for refusing to pay a fine ordered by the courts after she tried to name her baby 'Gesher', which means 'bridge'. Norwegians are only allowed to use names that appear on an approved list – and Gesher was not on it.

- **Find a name with meaning.** Choosing a name that has a backstory will help your child to understand their significance in the world so – whether you name them after a saint or prophet, an important political figure or a hero in a Greek tragedy – ensure that they know where their name came from. They may just be inspired to be as great as their namesake.

- **Have fun.** Picking out names should be fun. Laughing at the ones you'd never dream of choosing can really help you to narrow it down to the ones you would. You can also experiment with different spellings, pronunciations or variations of names you like.

- **Expand your mind.** Don't rule out the weird ones just yet! As a teenager, I went to school with a girl named Siam. Her parents had conceived her on a honeymoon trip to Thailand and gave her the country's old name as a result. She loved growing up and having an unusual name, as I'm sure Milan (Shakira and Gerard Piqué's son) and India (Chris Hemsworth and Elsa Pataky's daughter) do too. Also, don't be afraid to play around with spellings and pronunciations, which are trends that we've seen emerge. However, do be careful not to saddle your child with an impossible name to spell, pronounce and fit on a passport application form.

- **Try it out.** While you're pregnant, talk to your baby and address it by using a variety of your favourite names to see if it responds. There are numerous stories of names being chosen because the baby kicked when it was called Charlie or Aisha but was suspiciously silent when addressed as Dexter or Mildred, so see if yours has a preference! You can also try writing names down, practising a few signatures or saying one out loud enough times to see if you ever get sick of it.

- **Do NOT pick the name of an ex.** No matter how lovely Brad Pitt might have thought the name 'Jennifer' was, it's unlikely that Angelina Jolie would have allowed him to use it for one of their daughters. The same is probably true of picking the names of your friends' exes. They are unlikely to thank you if they have to say a name they loathe repeatedly. Just steer clear of any names you know will cause problems to other people, paying particular attention to your partner and loved ones.

- **What if you can't agree?** This is probably the trickiest problem to solve in the baby-naming process. It's wise to research a number of names in which you and your partner are both interested and make a point of discussing your reasons for liking or disliking them long before the baby is due to be born. The labour and delivery room are probably not the best time to discuss it! Avoid sticking to your guns on a name that one of you really doesn't like because it might lead to resentment down the line, with your baby caught in the middle. You could try compromising and picking two middle names so that you both have a name in there that you love or you could each have five names that you're allowed to 'veto' – but no more. You could also try considering contractions out of names you both like, such as Anna and Lisa (Annalisa) or James and Hayden (Jayden). Whichever way you go about it, it's important that you eventually agree on the name you are giving your baby, even if it means losing out on the one you've had your heart set on for a while.

- **Use apps.** With all the new technology literally at our fingertips, how about putting some of it to good use? There are hundreds of new apps for smartphones and tablets that promise to help you to narrow down the endless lists of potential names until you find the one you love.

> ❝ Always end the name of your child with a vowel, so that when you yell the name will carry. ❞
> Bill Cosby

Think to the future

One important aspect of naming your child is thinking ahead to their future. Will the name you've chosen stand the test of time? Will names popular in 2014 remain popular in 2040? Will they be able to enter a room and give a crucial business presentation confidently with an awkward or unpronounceable name? Even earlier on, can they survive the potential minefields of primary and secondary school with a name that could be easily shortened to something embarrassing?

An Icelandic girl won a 15-year battle in 2013 to keep her birth name after authorities originally deemed 'Blaer' too masculine for a girl. Finally, she is now free to use her real name, which means 'light breeze', on her passport and at school.

Names that should be banned – but aren't

Anna Banana Baptista

Benson and Hedges (twins)

Kaos

Laxative Thomas

Masport and Mower (twins)

Midnight Chardonnay Number 16 Bus Shelter

Spiral Cicada

Superman (changed from 4Real)

Violence

Stereotypes: true or false?

Will the name you choose actually affect your child's life?
Will names that seem clever mean that your child will be
brainier? Will names with positive meanings make your
child into a happier person? The answer is . . . possibly.

Some experts believe that parents who choose inspirational
names for their offspring (e.g. Destiny, Serenity, Unique)
or names of products they would like to own (e.g. Armani,
Jaguar, Mercedes) are projecting a future on to their child
for them to aspire to, thus helping to shape their life.
However, there's absolutely no evidence that this
actually works!

Inspirational names

Destiny	Joy
Happy	Peace
Heaven	Serenity
Hope	Unique
Innocence	Unity

Aspirational names

Armani	Ferrari
Aston	Jaguar
Bugatti	Mercedes
Chanel	Porsche
Dolce	Prada

One thing you should consider is how your child's name will be perceived by the outside world. Typically, judgements are passed on names, even before meeting a person, in situations such as job interviews or at school.

Last year, teachers across the country were asked to decide from a list of names which children were more likely to be badly behaved than others. Topping the 'naughty' charts were Callum, Connor and Jack for boys, and Chelsea, Courtney and Chardonnay for girls. On the other hand, the names in the 'clever' category were Alexander, Adam and Christopher for boys, and Elizabeth, Charlotte and Emma for girls.

Teachers were also asked to pick names that they felt were likely to be given to 'popular' children and these included Jack, Daniel, Charlie, Emma, Charlotte and Hannah – meaning that little boys named Jack are naughty but popular!

In a different survey, teachers were asked to pick names that they felt were particularly 'chavvy'. Chantelle, Jordan, Kylie and Paige came out on top for the girls, while Connor, Dwayne, Liam and Rhys were ranked first for the boys. Around the same time, it was discovered that teenagers named Katherine and Duncan (or a variation of the two, such as Kate) were up to eight times more likely to achieve high GCSE results than those named Wayne or Jermaine.

Another study analysed the number of stickers given to children as rewards for good behaviour. Those named Abigail and Jacob are more likely to be praised for being

well behaved than children named Beth and Josh;
moreover, kids who do not shorten their name or go by
nicknames are more likely to be better behaved, too.

Names which mean 'clever'

Abner	Shanahan
Cassidy	Todd
Haley	Ulysses
Penelope	Washington
Portia	Wylie

Names which sound 'clever'

Alastair	Gabriel
Charles	Harriet
Christian	Sophia
Elizabeth	Spencer
Frances	William

Children who are told that they have inherited an ancestor's
name or that of an influential character from history seem
to be more driven and focused than children who are told
disappointingly, 'We just liked the sound of it.' As a parent,
it seems it's okay to pick an unusual name if you have the
story or anecdotal evidence to back it up. Naming your
child Atticus (after Atticus Finch from Harper Lee's *To Kill A
Mockingbird*, known for being a strong and moral character)
may therefore not be a bad idea . . . However, there is no
actual scientific evidence to prove how the power of names
directly affects someone's life – it's all anecdotal.

Personality and character have a far greater influence than name alone and, after a while, a name becomes just a name.

Top 10 names in New Zealand

Boys	Girls
1. Jack	1. Olivia
2. Oliver	2. Sophie
3. William	3. Emily
4. Liam	4. Charlotte
5. Mason	5. Ruby
6. Samuel	6. Isabella
7. Jacob	7. Ella
8. Lucas	8. Amelia
9. Ethan	9. Sophia
10. Noah	10. Ava

Quirky names

There are lots of disadvantages to having a quirky name, but there are plenty of advantages, too. For one thing, your child's name will never be forgotten by other people, and if they do something influential with their life then their name could become an inspiration for other parents. On the other hand, a quirky name often requires a quirky personality. If you don't think your genes could stand up to a name like Satchel or Kerensa, perhaps it's time to think of one a little more run-of-the-mill.

What not to call your child

In Pennsylvania a few years ago there was a case of a supermarket bakery refusing to ice the words 'Happy Birthday, Adolf Hitler' on to a three-year-old's birthday cake. The parents were able to eventually fulfil the order at another shop but, as a result of the publicity surrounding the event, Social Services were called in to assess the child's home and Adolf was taken into care – along with his siblings Joycelynn Aryan Nation and Honszlynn Hinler Jeannie.

Controversial names adopted by real people

Adolf Hitler

Beelzebub

Desdemona

Hannibal Lecter

Himmler

Jezebel

Lucifer

Mussolini

Stalin

Voldemort

A survey carried out recently by the National Centre for Social Research found that the more unusual the name, the less likely a candidate is to be called for a job interview after submitting a CV. Whether or not this fact would affect a child's development and future career is yet to be determined, but it is something to consider.

Disease names throughout history

Rubella Graves (born 1814)

Cholera Priest (born 1830)

Emma Royd (born 1850)

Fever Bender (born 1856)

Hysteria Johnson (born 1881)

Mumps Sykes (born 1891)

Kathryn E. Coli (born 1894)

Typhus Black (born 1897)

Leper Priest (born 1929)

There is also new research from baby website Bounty, which says that as many as one in five parents regrets their choice of baby name. Of the 3,000 parents interviewed, 20% said they no longer thought the unusual choice of spelling or pronunciation was appropriate. Around 8% said they were tired of people mispronouncing their child's name and 10% thought the novelty of the original pick had worn off. They also said they would now pick a new name which had not occurred to them or been an option before.

Although parents are often discouraged from picking wild and crazy names for their babies (think about little Blue Ivy, Beyoncé's daughter, or Zuma Nesta Rock, Gwen Stefani's second son), there isn't actually any evidence to suggest that children are hindered in any way by them, unless they're really, really extreme.

Helen Fairey of Derby changed her name by deed poll to Christmas Fairy in 2010. She now works for a large hotel chain, ensuring guests have plenty of Christmas cheer every year.

Masculine vs feminine

How do we define what makes a name masculine or feminine? Well, it may be connected to the sounds that the letters create, either when written down or spoken aloud. Harder-sounding combinations (-ter, -it, -ld, -id) tend to be found in masculine names, whereas softer-sounding combinations (-ie, -ay, -la) are generally associated with feminine names. Therefore, you end up with Sophie, Joanie and Bella, and Harold, Walter and David.

If you're planning on choosing a feminine-sounding name, approach with caution: recent research suggests that girls who are given particularly 'girly' names – think Tiana, Kayla and Isabella – are much more likely to misbehave when they reach school age. These 'feminine' girls were also far less likely to choose subjects at school such as maths and science, while their sisters with more masculine names – for example, Morgan, Alexis and Ashley – were encouraged to excel in these courses.

Nowadays, names are becoming more androgynous and many appear in both boys' and girls' lists: Hayden, Riley, Madison and, of course, Alex – some form of which appears in the Top 100 for both boys and girls every year. Therefore, if you want a more gender-neutral name for your new arrival, you won't be alone.

Nicknames

" " Nicknames stick to people, and the most ridiculous are the most adhesive. " "

Thomas C. Haliburton

Nicknames are unavoidable. They can range from the common – such as Mike from Michael or Sam from Samantha – to the trendy, funny or downright insulting. As we saw earlier, there's a growing trend of parents using nicknames as their baby's full name and getting rid of the longer name altogether. If you're going to stick with the longer name, however, make sure that you're going to be happy with any nicknames that emerge.

The first time your child encounters a nickname will probably be before they are even born – or at least within the first few months. Many older siblings find new names hard to remember or pronounce and your baby could end up with a nickname before you know it. If your baby has an older sibling, try talking to them about their new brother or sister using the name you've picked so you can discover how their imagination might choose to interpret it. If they are an older child you might even want to include them in the naming process from the start, if for no other reason than they might mention a friend at school who gets teased for having an unfortunate nickname derived from the name you've chosen.

You can pre-empt problem nicknames to some extent by saying the name you've chosen out loud and trying to find rhymes for it. This is a clever way to avoid playground chants and nursery rhyme-type insults, such as Andy Pandy or Looby Lou. It's a sad truth, though, that children will rhyme anything with anything else if they can, so while you might wish to take playground chants into account during your naming process, don't be too concerned about them. Most children are subjected to it at some point and emerge unscathed.

French law prohibits all names other than those on an approved list. However, in 2012 French courts allowed one couple to call their child 'Daemon' after a vampire character in the TV show *The Vampire Diaries* called Damon – the first such deviation from the approved list in a decade.

Using family names

Some families have a strong tradition of using names that come from the family tree and therefore there are instances where naming your baby boy Augustine VIII is simply not just an option: it's a rule. Another way families do this is by giving children the name of their parent of the same sex and adding 'Junior' (Jr) to the end. This could only potentially create a problem if that child then decides to carry on the tradition and name their child after themselves – after all, who wants to be known as Frederick Jr Jr? Admittedly, this doesn't seem to happen very often in the UK but it is something to consider if it is one of your family's traditions. There are pros and cons with using family names.

- **Pro:** your child will feel part of a strong tradition, which will create a sense of security for them and help to make them feel a complete member of the family.

- **Pro:** if you're struggling to select a name that you and your partner both agree on, this is a very simple solution and will make your new child's family very happy.

- **Con:** you might not actually like the name that's being passed down. Naming your child the twelfth Thumbelina in a row might not actually hold the same attraction for you as for the generation before.

- **Con:** another drawback could be if the cultural associations with that name have changed in your lifetime and it is no longer appropriate.

Traditional names

Boys	Girls
Arthur	Ava
Charlie	Dorothy
Edward	Elizabeth
Fred	Grace
Harry	Louisa
Henry	Margaret
Joseph	Martha
Julian	Mary
Miles	Olivia
William	Rosemary

One way to navigate your way around choosing a family name is to compromise. You could use the name as a middle name or refer to your baby by a nickname instead. You could also suggest using a name from the other parent's family: if the name comes from your side, try finding one you like from the other side. If their argument is for tradition then this is an astonishingly effective counter-argument.

Spend a lot of time on social media? How about doing what one British family did in 2012 and naming your baby 'Hashtag'? Or you could copy the Egyptian baby called 'Facebook'.

Top 10 boys' names in 1914 and 1994

1914	1994
l. John	1. Thomas
2. William	2. James
3. George	3. Jack
4. Thomas	4. Daniel
5. James	5. Matthew
6. Arthur	6. Ryan
7. Frederick	7. Joshua
8. Albert	8. Luke
9. Charles	9. Samuel
10. Robert	10. Jordan

Whatever you decide to do with regard to using family names, just remember that this is your baby. Just as your parents got to decide what they named you, you get to decide this. If family and friends are disappointed, don't be alarmed. Once the baby is here, all they will see is how much she has her grandmother's nose or his grandfather's ears, and the name will become far less important.

Top 10 girls' names in 1914 and 1994

1914	1994
1. Mary	1. Rebecca
2. Margaret	2. Lauren
3. Doris	3. Jessica
4. Dorothy	4. Charlotte
5. Kathleen	5. Hannah
6. Florence	6. Sophie
7. Elsie	7. Amy
8. Edith	8. Emily
9. Elizabeth	9. Laura
10. Winifred	10. Emma

Spellings and pronunciation

Once you've finally agreed upon a name, it's time to think about how you wish it to be spelt and pronounced. Some parents love experimenting with unusual variations of traditional names, while others prefer names to be instantly recognisable. The only advice here is to use caution in your experiments. There are many hilarious tales of parents seeing or hearing what they think are pretty names in the hospital during delivery and choosing them for their children, only to find out later that they are medical terms and therefore completely inappropriate.

Medical terms used as names

The following list was provided by a practising midwife who has vivid recollections of parents thinking they were naming their children something unique and original, only to be told that the name they'd chosen was in fact a medical term.

Chlamydia (pronounced cler-mid-EE-ya)

Eczema (pronounced ex-SEE-mah)

Female (pronounced fuh-MAH-lee)

Latrine (pronounced lah-TREE-nee)

Meconium (pronounced meh-COH-nee-um)

Syphilis (pronounced see-PHIL-iss)

Testicles (pronounced TESS-tee-clees)

Urine (pronounced yer-REE-nee)

Vagina (pronounced vaj-EE-nah)

Obviously, the examples above are a little extreme, but the choices you make regarding spelling and pronunciation are really important. And, as we have seen a growing trend in parents coming up with their own spellings, it's even more important that you take note if you are thinking of doing that too!

Try to avoid making a common name too long or too unusual in its spelling, as this will be the first thing your child learns how to write. They will also be subjected to constant corrections during their lifetime, as other people misspell or mispronounce their name in ever more frustrating patterns. Also, make sure that the name isn't so long that it won't fit on forms or name badges, as they'll simply stop using it and take on a nickname instead. Substituting the odd 'i' for a 'y' isn't too bad, but turning the name Jonathan into Jonnaythanne doesn't do anyone any favours.

Pronunciation matters: a Swedish couple were once banned from naming their child 'Brfxxccxxmnpcccclllmmnprxvclmnckssqlbblll6', which they claimed was pronounced 'Albin'.

Britain has seen an increase in 'text' language spellings.

An	Jaicub
Camron	Jayk
Conna	Lora
Ema	Patryk
Esta	Samiul
Flicity	Summa
Helin	Wilym

Middle names

Giving your child a middle name is pretty standard practice these days. In fact, it has become fairly uncommon not to do so, although the use of second and third names only became popular around the turn of the twentieth century. Before then, giving a child a middle name was seen as a status symbol; it was only really used when a man married a higher-class woman and they wanted to keep the woman's

maiden name as a reminder of that child's heritage. Once
the fashion caught on, it became very popular to give more
than one middle name to children of status, but it's only
been since the 1900s that it became standard for everyone.

Regardless of your status, a middle name can have just as
much of an impact as a forename so your choice for your
baby should be made as carefully as the one for their first
name.

Sweden has a pretty strict naming law, enacted in
1982, which says: 'First names shall not be approved if
they can cause offence or can be supposed to cause
discomfort for the one using it, or names which for
some obvious reason are not suitable as a first name.'
However, they did recently approve the use of 'Google'
as a middle name.

You may have already decided what middle name to give
your child due to tradition or culture, in which case the
following advice may be moot. In Spanish culture, for
example, middle names are often the mother's surname or
other name to promote the matriarchal lineage. Similarly,
parents who have not taken each other's surnames or are
not married may choose to give their child one surname as
a middle name and one as a last name so that both parents
are represented. However, be aware that doing either of
these things can create some strange name combinations,
as Richard Tiffany Gere, Billie Paul Piper and Courtney
Bass Cox can testify. Other traditions may use an old family
name, passed down to each first-born son or daughter, to

encourage a sense of family pride and history. A decision about what middle name to pass on may have therefore already been made for you, even before your own birth.

Unique middle names are very much in vogue right now with celebrities, who are also using both the first and middle names all the time. Singer Bryan Adams and his partner Alicia Grimaldi call their new baby girl by her full name – Lulu Rosylea – as do Lily Allen and Sam Cooper with their daughter, Marnie Rose. And Fearne Cotton's little boy isn't just 'Rex': he's Rex Rayne.

Of course, there are always the stars who take trends and just run with them, using not only something wacky but also multiple names when one will do; ex-glamour model Holly Madison did that with her new addition: Rainbow Aurora. Holly has defended her choice, publicly saying:

> There are a lot of smug haters out there who bag on my choice of a name, but I don't care about what they think. I want my daughter to be proud of who she is and learn to speak up and stand up for herself at a young age.

If you are choosing a middle name, there are some common trends for 2014 to help you narrow it down.

- **Opposite-length names.** It has become very popular to give a child either a long forename and short middle name or a short forename and long middle name. If this idea attracts you, consider using syllables to give you an idea of length and combinations. Generally, if the forename has only one or two syllables (Owen, Steven, Yasmin, Zoe) then the middle name should have two, three or even four syllables (Owen Jonathan, Steven Michael, Yasmin Samantha, Zoe Jessica). If the opposite is true and the forename is three or four syllables long (Anthony, Jennifer, Nicholas, Rosemary) then the middle name may be better kept to only one or two syllables (Anthony Kevin, Jennifer Ruth, Nicholas John, Rosemary Dawn).

- **Names from the family tree.** Honouring your ancestors is another popular trend for 2014. Parents are frequently looking back to their own lineage for interesting, unusual or influential names.

The shortest baby names are only two letters long (Al, Ed, Jo, and Ty) but the longest could be any length imaginable. Popular 11-letter long names include Bartholomew, Christopher, Constantine and Maximillian.

- **Unusual names.** Along with a wider variety of first names recently (Ruby, Lexie and Mia have all climbed the Top 20 charts over the last few years), parents are choosing more unusual middle names too. This makes sense, as a child named Bronte or Keilyn probably needs a fairly uncommon middle name to balance it out. Alternatively, as middle names are far less frequently used, this is an opportunity for parents to have an unusual name included which they wouldn't perhaps have used otherwise. If their child grows up not to like it then they have the option of only using their initial, or simply dropping it from daily use altogether.

It is becoming increasingly common to use a parent's first name as a middle name.

Predicted popular middle names for 2014

Boys	Girls
Adam	Anne
Christopher	Elise
David	Elizabeth
Hugh	Grace
Jackson	Jane
Joseph	Leigh
Lee	Marie
Michael	May
Steven	Rose
Thomas	Ruth

As with first names, middle names can have hilarious consequences if not considered carefully. It's worth writing down your favourite combinations and saying them out loud to make sure you're not making one of these mistakes . . .

Amusing middle name combinations

Brandy Ann Koch (brandy and coke)

Claire Annette Reed (clarinet reed)

Harry Armand Bach (hairy arm and back)

Justin Miles North (just ten miles north)

Laura Lynne Hardy (Laurel and Hardy)

Lisa May Boyle (Lisa may boil)

Mary Annette Woodin (marionette wooden)

May Ann Naze (mayonnaise)

Norma Leigh Lucid (normally lucid)

Sam Ann Fisher (salmon fisher)

Of course, you don't have to narrow down middle name choices to just one. It is becoming increasingly common to have several middle names, particularly if parents like more than one or want to include a family name as well.

Be careful not to have too many, though, as this makes life very difficult when filling out official forms or enrolling your child in school. Most institutions only recognise one middle name and some only recognise a middle initial.

Some famous examples of multiple middle names include British musician Brian Eno, whose full name is actually Brian Peter George St. John le Baptiste de la Salle Eno, and Canadian actor Kiefer Sutherland, who has shortened his name considerably from Kiefer William Frederick Dempsey George Rufus Sutherland. Even the Royal Family likes to give many middle names: Prince Charles's full name is Charles Philip Arthur George Mountbatten-Windsor and Prince William is William Arthur Philip Louis Mountbatten-Windsor.

Bizarre baby names from the US

Boys	Girls
Aero	Ace
Burger	Kaixin
Donathan	Leeloo
Espn	Monalisa
Haven'T	Rogue
Kix	Sesame
Pawk	Thinn
Rysk	Yoga
Zaniel	Zealand

Many people actually choose to go by their middle name instead of their forename, so it could be seen as a safety net if you're worried that your child won't like their name. For example, Alyson Hannigan and Alexis Denisof have given their daughters, Satyana Marie and Keeva Jane, more traditional middle names as a way of counter-balancing their unusual first names, thus providing them with the option of switching to the more conventional option when they grow up.

Celebrities who go by middle names

Antonio Banderas (José Antonio Dominguez Banderas)
Ashton Kutcher (Christopher Ashton Kutcher)
Bob Marley (Nesta Robert Marley)
Brad Pitt (William Bradley Pitt)

Brooke Shields (Christa Brooke Camille Shields)

Dakota Fanning (Hannah Dakota Fanning)

Evangeline Lilly (Nicole Evangeline Lilly)

Hugh Laurie (James Hugh Calum Laurie)

Kelsey Grammar (Allen Kelsey Grammar)

Reese Witherspoon (Laura Jean Reese Witherspoon)

Rihanna (Robyn Rihanna Fenty)

Will Ferrell (John William Ferrell)

Long, longer and longest

How about trying to beat the record for the world's longest name? The Glastonbury teenager named Captain Fantastic Faster Than Superman Spiderman Batman Wolverine Hulk And The Flash Combined changed his name from George Garratt in 2008. At the time, he claimed to have the longest name in the world, replacing Texan woman Rhoshandiatellyneshiaunneveshenk Koyaanisquatsiuth Williams, whose 57-letter long name paled in comparison to Captain's 81 letters. However, a woman from Hartlepool beat both these records in 2012, when she changed her name by Legal Deed Poll from Dawn McManus to . . . and get ready for this: Red Wacky League Antlez Broke the Stereo Neon Tide Bring Back Honesty Coalition Feedback Hand of Aces Keep Going Captain Let's Pretend Lost State of Dance Paper Taxis Lunar Road Up Down Strange All And I Neon Sheep Eve Hornby Faye Bradley AJ Wilde Michael Rice Dion Watts

Matthew Appleyard John Ashurst Lauren Swales Zoe Angus Jaspreet Singh Emma Matthews Nicola Brown Leanne Pickering Victoria Davies Rachel Burnside Gil Parker Freya Watson Alisha Watts James Pearson Jacob Sotheran Darley Beth Lowery Jasmine Hewitt Chloe Gibson Molly Farquhar Lewis Murphy Abbie Coulson Nick Davies Harvey Parker Kyran Williamson Michael Anderson Bethany Murray Sophie Hamilton Amy Wilkins Emma Simpson Liam Wales Jacob Bartram Alex Hooks Rebecca Miller Caitlin Miller Sean McCloskey Dominic Parker Abbey Sharpe Elena Larkin Rebecca Simpson Nick Dixon Abbie Farrelly Liam Grieves Casey Smith Liam Downing Ben Wignall Elizabeth Hann Danielle Walker Lauren Glen James Johnson Ben Ervine Kate Burton James Hudson Daniel Mayes Matthew Kitching Josh Bennett Evolution Dreams. Red (formerly Dawn) changed her name to this 161-word whopper to raise money for her charity, Red Dreams (now her first and last name), set up after the death of her son.
And yes, she really did it!

Perhaps the longest celeb baby name for a while: Uma Thurman's daughter, Rosalind Arusha Arkadina Altalune Florence Thurman-Busson, was born in July 2012.

Initials

What surname will your baby have? Does its first letter lend itself easily to amusing acronyms already? And would choosing certain forenames only exacerbate the problem?

If your child will inherit a double-barrelled surname this becomes a bigger consideration still, as there are more amusing four-letter words than there are three-letter ones. My brother-in-law was going to be called Andrew Steven Schmitt before he was born, until his parents realised at the last minute what his initials would spell . . .

The website Name of The Year pronounced a Dutch pharmacoepidemiologist as the winner of their annual competition last year: Taco B. M. Monster. He beat Monquarius Mungo, Atticus Disney and La'Peaches Pitts to win the top spot.

It's worth taking the time to think about the acronyms formed by initials in the real world too, such as how names are displayed on credit cards or imagining your child's name written out on a form. Nobody should have to go through life known as S. Lugg because their parents didn't think that far ahead.

Amusing initials

Al E. Gador	I.C. Blood
Angie O. Graham	I. P. Freely
Earl E. Bird	Kay F. Cee
Gene E. Yuss	S. Lugg
H. I. Vee	Warren T.

> "I call everyone 'darling' because I can't remember their names."

Zsa Zsa Gabor

Amusing acronyms of real people

David Vernon Durante – DVD

George Barry Holmes – GBH

Jake Clive Baxter – JCB

James John Brookes – JJB (the sportswear shop)

Jennifer Paige Garrett – JPG

Neil Christopher Parker – NCP (the car park)

Patricia Mary Simpson – PMS

Sally Theresa Donaghue – STD

Samuel Alan Spencer – SAS

Victoria Helen Smith – VHS

Across the UK, there are people whose initials spell out three-letter words – from RAT and FAG to FAB or POP – and some are better than others, so do check!

Your surname

Tied to your child's potential new initials is their new surname. Whether they are receiving their name from their mother, father or a hyphenated combination of both, matching an appropriate first name to their surname is an important undertaking. In order to prevent a lifetime of embarrassment for your baby, try to avoid forenames that might lead to unfortunate outcomes when combined with certain surnames. The best way to work out whether this might happen is to write down all the names you like alongside your child's last name and have someone else read them out loud. This second pair of eyes and ears might just spot something that you didn't.

Unfortunate first name/surname combinations

Anna Sasin	Jenny Taylor
Barb Dwyer	Justin Time
Barry Code	Mary Christmas
Ben Dover	Oliver Sutton
Duane Pipe	Paige Turner
Grace Land	Russell Sprout
Harry Rump	Stan Still
Hazel Nutt	Teresa Green
Isabella Horn	

The age of the internet has given parents a wonderful new weapon in their baby-naming arsenal: the search engine. Before you settle on anything final, try searching for any examples of the complete first name, middle name and surname of your new baby. You may find out that your baby has an axe-murderer namesake or, like one of my colleagues, the same name as a well-known porn star.

There is also the danger of your child being subjected to having a spoonerism made out of their name, where the first letters or syllables get swapped around to form new words. Named after the Reverend Dr William Archibald Spooner (1844–1930), a spoonerism can be created out of almost anything to make clever, amusing or downright inappropriate phrases instead. An unfortunate and recent example of this would be Angelina Jolie and Brad Pitt's daughter Shiloh, whom they named Shiloh Jolie-Pitt to avoid the inevitable Shiloh Pitt spoonerism. Try to avoid making the same mistake!

Twitter became a hot spot for spoonerisms, with celebrities such as Justin Bieber and Nick Jonas reportedly calling each other 'Bustin Jieber' and 'Jick Nonas'. After all, no one ever said spoonerisms have to make sense . . .

Celebrity spoonerisms

Gene Kelly (keen jelly)

Gordon Brown (broaden gown)

Justin Bieber (bustin jieber)

Jude Law (lewd jaw)

Kelly Brook (belly crook)

Mike Baker (bike maker)

Nick Jonas (jick nonas)

Sarah Palin (para sailing)

Shiloh Pitt (pile o' s***)

Shirley Bassey (burly chassis)

Paul Walker (wall porker)

Wesley Snipes (snesley wipes)

German law prohibits invented and androgynous names but the UK has some of the most liberal rules on naming a baby in the world, with only names which are deemed to be offensive making it on to the banned list.

4

Registering a baby's name

There are slightly different guidelines for registering births and names depending on where you live in the UK.

In England, Wales and Northern Ireland a birth must be recorded within 42 days of delivery and if not done at the hospital it requires a visit to a register office.

The birth certificate will be written in English, if a child is born in England or Northern Ireland, and can be in both English and Welsh if they are born in Wales.

If the birth is recorded at the hospital or registered in the same district then birth certificates are usually issued straightaway but if you end up going to a different office, the certificate may be sent to you after a few days. This is important when applying for Child Benefit or registering your baby with a doctor, as you will need a copy of the short birth certificate to apply.

> 66 Names are not always what they seem. The common Welsh name BZJXXLLWCP is pronounced Jackson. 99
>
> Mark Twain

If the parents of a newborn are married, either parent can register a birth. However, if the parents are not married there are several ways to ensure that both names are put on the birth certificate, including both parents being physically present at the registration or one parent submitting a declaration form in lieu of their presence. If neither parent can be present then someone who was present at the birth or someone who is now responsible for the child can also carry out the duty.

After the registration, the parents or those with parental responsibility also have the option of requesting a naming ceremony. These non-religious ceremonies are conducted by local authorities and can be a nice replacement for a baptism or christening, as adults outside of the family can be nominated to act in secular roles similar to godparents. A birth certificate is also needed for this event to take place.

In Scotland births need to be registered within 21 days and can take place in any district. As well as either married parent being allowed to register the birth, their relatives may also do the duty. The exception here is if the parents are not married. In this case the father may only register the birth if the mother is also present, a declaration form is submitted or a court agrees that he has parental responsibility just like any other adult. Parents of newborns in Scotland should take a card given to them at the hospital and a copy of their marriage certificate to the birth registration.

If you decide at a later stage that you want to change details on the birth certificate then there are procedures in place to help, although it is often a time-consuming process.

Useful websites for registering a birth

In England and Wales: www.gov.uk
In Northern Ireland: www.nidirect.gov.uk
In Scotland: www.gro-scotland.gov.uk

It is worth remembering that if the father's details were not recorded on the original certificate or if the natural parents have married since the registration, a new birth certificate will have to be generated. Both changes require filling out an application form, available on the websites listed above.

If you are unhappy with the forename you've chosen or it has been spelt incorrectly, you can change the birth record providing you have other documentation to prove this is the case. A passport or baptismal certificate is sufficient, as they will show the correct spelling or commonly used forename and should be presented to the register office where the initial application was made.

Changing the surname of your baby is only possible in two cases: either when the spelling is incorrect or if the details of the parents are being changed (such as the inclusion of the father or the parents now being married). Again, evidence and form submissions are needed to make any alterations and a fee is usually incurred if a new certificate is required.

In 2011 the then-Pope Benedict decreed all names should come from the Christian calendar. Italy promptly forbade one couple from naming their child 'Venerdî' ('Friday') because it would open the boy up to ridicule and mockery. The parents threatened to name their next son 'Mercoledî' ('Wednesday') in response.

Keep in mind how difficult it may be for you to change your child's birth certificate at a later stage if you are in any way unsure about the choice you're about to make. However, also remember that if something unexpected happens and you need to make the change, it is possible. There are stories of drunken fathers registering the birth of their child on their own and choosing a name that had not been agreed upon by the mother, much to her horror. As Robert Eisenschmidt said, 'I have a friend, Bill Land, who named his daughter Alison Wanda Land. His wife changed the name on the birth certificate when she found out.' So it is possible, though obviously not preferred.

Popular names in South Africa

Boys	Girls
Abrahem	Abri
Baruti	Dikeledi
Dingane	Jacoline
Fenyang	Kagiso
Lefu	Limpho
Letsego	Mosa
Moswen	Nobanzi
Nku	Nomuula
Tau	Siphiwe
Uuka	Tale

5

Naming twins, triplets, and more

If you have discovered you are expecting multiples, congratulations! Naming multiples needn't be any different to naming a single child . . . unless you want it to be. You could stick to the same process as everyone else by picking a unique name for each child. Even 'Octomom' Nadya Suleman chose eight different names for her octuplets, although they do all sound reasonably similar: Isaiah, Jeremiah, Jonah, Josiah, Maliah, McCai, Nariah and Noah.

Another option is to go with a theme. Try anagrams, names in reverse or giving each child the same initials. You could do this even if you're not expecting multiples, like the

Duggar family of Arkansas, US, who have given each of their 19 children the initial 'J': Joshua, Jana, John David, Jill, Jessa, Jinger, Joseph, Josiah, Joy-Anna, Jedidiah, Jeremiah, Jason, James, Justin, Jackson, Johannah, Jennifer, Jordyn-Grace and Josie. Their latest arrival was named Jubilee, although she sadly passed away in late 2011. Eldest son Joshua is currently expecting his third child with wife Anna and so far their children all have names beginning with 'M'.

Some parents do like to use a theme, though, such as going down the alphabet (think Alastair, Benjamin, Christopher and David) or doing what the famous acting Phoenix clan did and giving each child a name to do with nature: River, Rain, Joaquin (Leaf), Liberty and Summer.

The UK's biggest family title is currently held by the Radfords. Sue and Noel Radford have not chosen to follow a theme when naming their 16 children, though: from oldest to youngest they are: Chris, Sophie, Chloe, Jack, Daniel, Luke, Millie, Katie, James, Ellie, Aimee, Josh, Max, Tilly May, Oscar and baby Caspar. They even have their first grandchild: Daisy.

A Texan woman gave birth to two sets of identical twin boys on the same day in 2013. Conceived naturally, the chances of which is one in 70 million, Tress and Manuel Montalvo named their miracles Ace, Blaine, Cash and Dylan (ABCD).

Mariah Carey and Nick Cannon chose to use names starting with the same letter for their twins. Before announcing their choices, Nick posted a clue to the names on Twitter:

'So we r bout 2 reveal the actual names and b4 we tell em 2 our friends etc. both begin w/M's!!!!' The couple then announced the arrival of Monroe and Moroccan Scott, girl and boy twins. 'Scott' is the same middle name as Nick Cannon and his grandmother's maiden name, and as Mariah Carey doesn't have a middle name, they skipped one for Monroe too.

A palindrome name is a name that is spelt the same backwards and forwards, as with Bob, Elle, Eve and Hannah.

Twin names with the same meaning

Bernard and Brian (strong)

Daphne and Laura (laurel)

Deborah and Melissa (bee)

Dorcas and Tabitha (gazelle)

Elijah and Joel (God)

Eve and Zoe (life)

Irene and Salome (peace)

Lucius and Uri (light)

Lucy and Helen (light)

Sarah and Almira (princess)

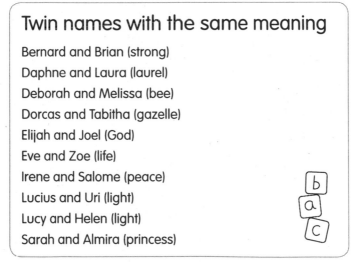

Popular twin names for 2014

Daniel and David
Ella and Emma
Gabriella and Isabella
Isaac and Isaiah
Jacob and Joshua
Madison and Morgan
Taylor and Tyler

Of course, when all is said and done, you can just stick to giving each child a name unique to them. For triplets, quads and more, this is probably an easier choice than twisting your head around three names with the same meaning or trying to create four anagrams you like for all of your babies.

Names for triplets

Aidan, Diana and Nadia (anagrams)
Amber, Jade and Ruby (jewels)
Amy, May and Mya (anagrams)
Ava, Eva and Iva (similar)
Daisy, Lily and Rose (flowers)
Jay, Raven and Robin (birds)
Olive, Violet and Sage (colours)
River, Rain and Summer (nature)

Celebrity twin names of the past few years

Darby and Sullivan (Patrick Dempsey and Jillian Fink)

D'Lila Star and Jessie James (P Diddy and Kim Porter)

Eddy and Nelson (Celine Dion and René Angélil)

Eden and Savannah (Marcia Cross and Tom Mahoney)

Hazel and Phinnaeus (Julia Roberts and Danny Moder)

Marion Loretta and Tabitha Hodge (Sarah Jessica Parker and Matthew Broderick)

Max and Bob (Charlie Sheen and Brooke Mueller)

Max and Emme (Jennifer Lopez and Marc Anthony)

Monroe and Moroccan Scott (Mariah Carey and Nick Cannon)

Vivienne Marcheline and Knox Leon (Angelina Jolie and Brad Pitt)

> 66 Names, once they are in common use, quickly become mere sounds, their etymology being buried, like so many of the earth's marvel beneath the dust of habit. 99

Salman Rushdie

part two

Boys' Names

 Boys' names

Aaron
Hebrew, meaning 'mountain of strength'.

Abasi
Egyptian, meaning 'male'.

Abdiel
Biblical, meaning 'servant of God'.

Abdul
Arabic, meaning 'servant'. Often followed with a suffix indicating who Abdul is the servant of (e.g. Abdul-Basit, 'servant of the creator').

Abdullah
Arabic, meaning 'servant of God'.

Abe
Hebrew, from Abraham, meaning 'father'.

Abel
Hebrew, meaning 'breath' or 'breathing spirit'. Associated with the biblical son of Adam and Eve who was killed by his brother Cain.

Abelard
German, meaning 'resolute'.

Aberforth
Gaelic, meaning 'mouth of the river Forth'.

A

Abheek
Indian, meaning 'fearless'.

Abhishek
Indian, meaning 'bath for a deity' or 'anointing'.

Abner
Hebrew, meaning 'father of light'.

Absalom
(alt. *Absalon*)
Hebrew, meaning 'father/ leader of peace'.

Acacio
Greek, meaning 'thorny tree'. Now widely used in Spain.

Ace
English, meaning 'number one' or 'the best'.

Achilles
Greek, mythological hero of the Trojan war, whose heel was his only weak spot.

Achim
Hebrew, meaning 'God will establish' or Polish, meaning 'the Lord exalts'.

Ackerley
Old English, meaning 'oak meadow'. Often used as a surname.

Adalberto
Germanic/Spanish, meaning 'nobly bright'.

Adam
Hebrew, meaning 'man' or 'earth'. First man to walk the earth, accompanied by Eve.

Adão
Variant of Adam, meaning 'earth'.

Addison
Old English, meaning 'son of Adam'. Also used as a female name in the US.

Ade
African, meaning 'peak' or 'pinnacle'.

Adelard

Teutonic, meaning 'brave' or 'noble'.

Adelbert

Old German form of Albert.

Aden

Gaelic, meaning 'fire'.

Adetokunbo

Yoruba, meaning 'the crown came from over the sea'.

Adin

Hebrew, meaning 'slender' or 'voluptuous'. Also Swahili, meaning 'ornamental'.

Aditya

Sanskrit, meaning 'belonging to the sun'.

Adlai

Hebrew, meaning 'God is just', or sometimes 'ornamental'.

Adler

Old German, meaning 'eagle'.

Adley

English, meaning 'son of Adam'.

Admon

Hebrew, variant of Adam meaning 'earth'. Also the name of a red peony.

Adolph

(alt. Adolf)

Old German, meaning 'noble majestic wolf'.

Adonis

Phoenician, meaning 'Lord'.

Adrian

Latin, meaning 'from Hadria', a town in northern Italy.

Movie inspirations

Austin *(Austin Powers)*
Don *(Singin' in the Rain)*
Edward (Twilight series)
Harry (Harry Potter series)
Jacob (Twilight series)
Jake *(Avatar)*
Kirk (Star Trek series)
Korben *(The Fifth Element)*
Marty *(Back to the Future)*
Michael *(The Godfather)*
Renton *(Trainspotting)*
Wayne *(Wayne's World)*

A

Adriel
Hebrew, meaning 'of God's flock'.

Adyn
(alt. Adann, Ade, Aden)
Irish, meaning 'manly'.

Aeneas
Greek/Latin, meaning 'to praise'. Name of the hero who founded Rome in Virgil's *Aeneid*.

Aero
Greek, meaning 'air'.

Aeson
Greek, father of Jason in Greek mythology.

Afonso
Portuguese, meaning 'eager noble warrior'.

Agamemnon
Greek, meaning 'leader of the assembly'. Figure in mythology, commanded the Greeks at the siege of Troy.

Agathon
Greek, meaning 'good' or 'superior'.

Agustin
Latin/Spanish, meaning 'venerated'.

Ahab
Hebrew, meaning 'father's brother'. Name of the obsessed captain in *Moby Dick*.

Ahijah
Hebrew, meaning 'brother of God' or 'friend of God'.

Ahmed
Arabic/Turkish, meaning 'worthy of praise'.

Aidan
(alt. Aiden)
Gaelic, meaning 'little fire'.

Aidric
Old English, meaning 'oaken'.

Airyck
Old Norse, from Eric, meaning 'eternal ruler'.

Ajani

African, meaning 'he fights for what he is'. Also Sanskrit, meaning 'of noble birth'.

Ajax

Greek, meaning 'mourner of the Earth'. Another Greek hero from the siege of Troy.

Ajay

Indian, meaning 'unconquerable'.

Ajit

Indian, meaning 'invincible'.

Akeem

Arabic, meaning 'wise or insightful'.

Akio

Japanese, meaning 'bright man'.

Akira

Japanese, meaning 'intelligent'.

Akiva

Hebrew, meaning 'to protect' or 'to shelter'.

Akon

American, meaning 'flower'. Made popular by the famous rapper charting in 2008/2009.

Aksel

Hebrew/Danish, meaning 'father of peace'.

Aladdin

Arabic, meaning 'servant of Allah'. From the medieval story in *Arabian Nights*.

Alan

(alt. Allan, Allen, Allyn, Alun)
Gaelic, meaning 'rock'.

Alaric

Old German, meaning 'noble regal ruler'.

Alastair

(alt. Alasdair, Allister)
Greek/Gaelic, meaning 'defending men'.

Alban

Latin, meaning 'from Alba'. Also the name of Saint Alban, the first British Christian martyr.

A

Alberic

Germanic, meaning 'Elfin king'.

Albert

Old German, meaning 'noble, bright, famous'.

Albin

Latin, meaning 'white'.

Albus

Latin, variant of Albin meaning 'white'.

Alcaeus

Greek, meaning 'strength'.

Alden

Old English, meaning 'old friend'.

Aldis

English, meaning 'from the old house'.

Aldo

Italian, meaning 'old' or 'elder'.

Aldric

English, meaning 'old King'.

Alec

(alt. Alek)

English, meaning 'defending men'.

Aled

Welsh, meaning 'child' or 'offspring'.

Aleph

Hebrew, meaning 'first letter of the alphabet', or 'leader'.

Aleron

(alt. Aileron, Alerun, Ailerun, Alejandro)

Latin, meaning 'child with wings'.

Alessio

Italian, meaning 'defender'.

Alexander

(alt. Alexandro, Alessandro, Alejandro)

Greek, meaning 'defending men'.

Alexei

Russian, meaning 'defender'.

Alfie

(alt. Alfi)

Shortened form of Alfred meaning 'elf'.

A

Alfonso

Germanic/Spanish, meaning 'noble and prompt, ready to struggle'.

Alford

Old English, meaning 'old river/ford'.

Alfred

(alt. Alf)

English, meaning 'elf' or 'magical counsel'.

Algernon

French, meaning 'with a moustache'.

Ali

(alt. Allie)

Arabic, meaning 'noble, sublime'.

Alois

German, meaning 'famous warrior'.

Alok

Indian, meaning 'cry of triumph'.

Alon

Jewish, meaning 'oak tree'.

Alonso

(alt. Alonzo)

Germanic, meaning 'noble and ready'.

Aloysius

Italian saint's name, meaning 'fame and war'.

Alpha

First letter of the Greek alphabet.

Alphaeus

Hebrew, meaning 'changing'.

Alpin

Gaelic, meaning 'related to the Alps'.

Altair

Arabic, meaning 'flying' or 'bird'.

Alter

Yiddish, meaning 'old man'.

Alton

Old English, meaning 'old town'.

Alva

Latin, meaning 'white'.

A

Alvie

German, meaning 'army of elves'.

Alvin

English, meaning 'friend of elves'.

Alwyn

Welsh, meaning 'wise friend'. May also come from the River Alwen in Wales.

Amachi

African, meaning 'who knows what God has brought us through this child'.

Amadeus

Latin, meaning 'God's love'.

Amadi

African, meaning 'appeared destined to die at birth'.

Amado

Spanish, meaning 'God's love'.

Amador

Spanish, meaning 'one who loves'.

Amari

Hebrew, meaning 'given by God'.

Amarion

Arabic, meaning 'populous, flushing'.

Amasa

Hebrew, meaning 'burden'.

Ambrose

Greek, meaning 'undying, immortal'.

Americo

Germanic, meaning 'ever powerful in battle'.

Amias

Latin, meaning 'loved'.

Amil

African, meaning 'effective'.

Amir

Hebrew, meaning 'prince' or 'treetop'.

Amit

Hindu, meaning 'friend'.

Ammon

Egyptian, meaning 'the hidden one'.

Amory

German/English, meaning 'work' and 'power'.

Amos

Hebrew, meaning 'encumbered' or 'burdened'.

Anacletus

Latin, meaning 'called back' or 'invoked'.

Anakin

American, meaning 'warrior'. Made famous by Anakin Skywalker in the Star Wars films.

Ananias

Greek/Italian, meaning 'answered by the Lord'.

Anastasius

Latin, meaning 'resurrection'.

Anat

Jewish, meaning 'water spring'.

Anatole

Greek, meaning 'cynical but without malice'.

Anders

Greek, meaning 'lion man'.

Anderson

English, meaning 'male'.

Andrew

(alt. Andreas)

Greek, meaning 'man' or 'warrior'.

Androcles

Greek, meaning 'glory of a warrior'.

Angel

(alt. Angelo)

Greek, meaning 'messenger'.

Angus

Scottish, meaning 'one choice'.

Anil

Sanskrit, meaning 'air' or 'wind'.

Anselm

German, meaning 'helmet of God'.

A

Anson
English, meaning 'son of Agnes'.

Anthony
English, from the old Roman family name.

Antipas
Israeli, meaning 'for all or against all'.

Antwan
Old English, meaning 'flower'.

Apollo
Greek, meaning 'to destroy'. Greek god of the sun.

Apostolos
Greek, meaning 'apostle'.

Ara
Armenian. Ara was a legendary king.

Aragorn
Literary, used by Tolkien in *The Lord of the Rings* trilogy.

Aram
Hebrew, meaning 'Royal Highness'.

Aramis
Latin, meaning 'swordsman'.

Arcadio
Greek/Spanish, from a place in ancient Greece. The word 'Arcadia' (meaning paradise) comes from this.

Archibald
(alt. Archie)
Old German, meaning 'genuine, bold, brave'.

Ardell
Latin, meaning 'eager, burning with enthusiasm'.

Arden
Celtic, meaning 'high'.

Ares
Greek, meaning 'ruin'. Son of Zeus and Greek god of war.

A

Ari

Hebrew, meaning 'lion' or 'eagle'.

Arias

Germanic, meaning 'lion'.

Aric

English, meaning 'merciful ruler'.

Ariel

Hebrew, meaning 'lion of God'. One of the archangels, the angel of healing and new beginnings.

Arild

Old Norse, meaning 'battle commander'.

Aris

Greek, meaning 'best figure'.

Ariston

Greek, meaning 'the best'.

Aristotle

Greek, meaning 'best'. Also a famous philosopher.

Arjun

Sanskrit, meaning 'white'.

Arkady

Greek, region of central Greece.

Arlan

Gaelic, meaning 'pledge' or 'oath'.

Arlie

Old English place name, meaning 'eagle wood'.

Arlis

Hebrew, meaning 'pledge'.

Arlo

Spanish, meaning 'barberry tree'.

Armand

Old German, meaning 'soldier'.

Armani

Same origin as Armand meaning 'soldier'.

A

Arnaldo
Spanish, meaning 'eagle power'.

Arnav
Indian, meaning 'the sea'.

Arnold
Old German, meaning 'eagle ruler'.

Arrow
English, from the common word denoting weaponry.

Art
Irish, name of a warrior in Irish mythology, Art Oenfer (Art the Lonely).

Arthur
(alt. Artie, Artis)
Celtic, probably from 'artos', meaning 'bear'. Made famous by the tales of King Arthur and the Knights of the Round Table.

Arvel
From the Welsh 'Arwel', meaning 'wept over'.

Arvid
English, meaning 'eagle in the woods'.

Arvind
Indian, meaning 'red lotus'.

Arvo
Finnish, meaning 'value' or 'worth'.

Arwen
Welsh, meaning 'fair' or 'fine'.

Asa
Hebrew, meaning 'doctor' or 'healer'.

Asante
African, meaning 'thank you'.

Asher
Hebrew, meaning 'fortunate' or 'lucky'.

Ashley
Old English, meaning 'ash meadow'.

Ashok
Sanskrit, meaning 'not causing sorrow'.

A

Ashton

English, meaning 'settlement in the ash-tree grove'.

Aslan

Turkish, meaning 'lion'. Strongly associated with the lion from C. S. Lewis' *The Lion, the Witch, and the Wardrobe*.

Asriel

Hebrew, meaning 'help of God'.

Astrophel

Latin, meaning 'star lover'.

Athanasios

Greek, meaning 'eternal life'.

Atílio

Portuguese, meaning 'father'.

Atlas

Greek, meaning 'to carry'. In Greek mythology Atlas was a Titan forced to carry the weight of the heavens.

Atlee

Hebrew, meaning 'God is just'.

Atticus

Latin, meaning 'from Athens'.

Auberon

Old German, meaning 'royal bear'.

Aubrey

Old German, meaning 'power'.

Auden

Old English, meaning 'old friend'.

Audie

Old English, meaning 'noble strength'.

Long names

Alexander
Bartholomew
Christopher
Demetrius
Giovanni
Montgomery
Obadiah
Roberto
Salvatore
Zachariah

A

Augustas
(alt. Augustus)
Latin, meaning 'venerated'.

Aurelien
French, meaning 'golden'.

Austin
Latin, meaning 'venerated'.
Also a city in the state of Texas
in the US.

Avery
(alt. Avrie, Averey, Averie)
English, meaning 'wise ruler'.

Avi
Hebrew, meaning 'father of a
multitude of nations'.

Awnan
Irish, meaning 'little Adam'.

Axel
Hebrew, meaning 'father is
peace'. Made famous by Guns
'n' Roses front man Axl Rose.

Ayers
(alt. Ayer, Aires, Aire)
English, meaning 'heir to a
fortune'.

Azarel
Hebrew, meaning 'helped by
God'.

Azaryah
Hebrew, meaning 'helped by
God'.

Azriel
Hebrew, meaning 'God is my
help'.

Azuko
African, meaning 'past glory'.

Boys' names

Baden

German, meaning 'battle'.

Bailey

English, meaning 'bailiff'.

Baird

Scottish, meaning 'poet' or 'one who sings ballads'.

Bakari

Swahili, meaning 'hope' or 'promise'.

Baker

English, from the word 'baker'.

Baldwin

Old French, meaning 'bold, brave friend'.

Balin

Old English. Balin was one of the Knights of the Round Table.

Balthazar

Babylonian, meaning 'protect the King'.

Balvinder

Hindu, meaning 'merciful, compassionate'.

Bannon

Irish, meaning 'descendant of O'Banain'. Also a river in Wales.

Barack

African, meaning 'blessed'. Made popular by US President Barack Obama.

B

Barclay

Old English, meaning 'birch tree meadow'. Also Persian, meaning 'messenger'.

Barker

Old English, meaning 'shepherd'.

Barnaby
(alt. Barney)

Greek, meaning 'son of consolation'.

Barnard

English, meaning 'strong as a bear'.

Baron

Old English, meaning 'young warrior'.

Barrett

English, meaning 'strong as a bear'.

Barron

Old German, meaning 'old clearing'.

Barry

Irish Gaelic, meaning 'fair haired'. Also a town in South Wales, made popular by the BBC TV series *Gavin and Stacey*.

Bart

Hebrew, from Bartholomew, meaning 'son of the farmer'.

Barton

Old English, meaning 'barley settlement'.

Baruch

Hebrew, meaning 'blessed'.

Barzillai

Hebrew, meaning 'my iron'.

Bashir

Arabic, meaning 'well-educated' and 'wise'.

Basil

Greek, meaning 'royal, kingly'.

B

Basim

Arabic, meaning 'smile'.

Bastien

Greek, meaning 'revered'.

Baxter

Old English, meaning 'baker'.

Bayard

French, meaning 'auburn haired'.

Bayre

American, meaning 'beautiful'.

Bayo

Nigerian, meaning 'to find joy'.

Biblical names

Abel
Cain
Eli
Jesus
Joseph
Luke
Mark
Moses
Paul
Peter
Solomon

Baz

Irish Gaelic, meaning 'fair-haired'.

Beau

French, meaning 'handsome'.

Beck

Old Norse, meaning 'stream'.

Beckett

Old English, meaning 'beehive' or 'bee cottage'. Associated with the Irish writer Samuel Beckett.

Beckham

English, meaning 'homestead by the stream'. Made famous by David and Victoria Beckham.

Béla

Hungarian, meaning 'within'.

Belarius

Shakespearean, meaning 'a banished lord'.

Benedict

Latin, meaning 'blessed'.

B

Benicio
Spanish, meaning 'benevolent'.

Benjamin
(alt. Ben)
Hebrew, meaning 'son of the south'.

Bennett
French/Latin vernacular form of Benedict, meaning 'blessed'.

Benoit
French form of Benedict, meaning 'blessed'.

Benson
English, meaning 'son of Ben'. Also linked to the village of Benson in Oxfordshire.

Bentley
Old English, meaning 'bent grass meadow'.

Benton
Old English, meaning 'town in the bent grass'.

Beriah
Hebrew, meaning 'in fellowship' or 'in envy'.

Bernard
(alt. Bernie)
Germanic, meaning 'strong, brave bear'.

Berry
Old English, meaning 'berry'.

Bert
(alt. Bertram/Bertrand)
Old English, meaning 'illustrious'.

Berton
Old English, meaning 'bright settlement'.

Bevan
Welsh, meaning 'son of Evan'.

Bilal
Arabic, meaning 'wetting, refreshing'.

Bill
(alt. Billy)
English, from William, meaning 'determined' or 'resolute'.

Birch
Old English, meaning 'bright' or 'shining'.

Birger

Norwegian, meaning 'rescue'.

Bishop

Old English, meaning 'bishop'.

Bjorn

Old Norse, meaning 'bear'.

Bladen

Hebrew, meaning 'hero'.

Blaine

Irish Gaelic, meaning 'yellow'.

Blair

English, meaning 'plain'.

Blaise

French, meaning 'lisp' or 'stutter'.

Blake

Old English, meaning 'dark, black'.

Blas

(alt. Blaze)

German, meaning 'firebrand'.

Bo

Scandinavian, short form of Robert, meaning 'bright fame'.

Boaz

Hebrew, meaning 'swiftness' or 'strength'.

Bob

(alt. Bobby)

Old German, from Robert meaning 'bright fame'.

Boden

(alt. Bodie)

Scandinavian, meaning 'shelter'.

Bogumil

Slavic, meaning 'God's favour'.

Bolivar

Spanish, meaning 'the bank of the river'.

Bond

Old English, meaning 'peasant farmer'.

Boris

Slavic, meaning 'battle glory'.

B

Saints' names

Aidan
Bernard
Francis
Gabriel
Kieran
Nicholas
Patrick
Stephen
Thomas
Vincent

Bosten

English, meaning 'town by the woods'.

Botolf

English, meaning 'wolf'.

Bowen

Welsh, meaning 'son of Owen'.

Boyd

Scottish Gaelic, meaning 'yellow'.

Brad
(alt. Bradley)

Old English, meaning 'broad' or 'wide'.

Brady

Irish, meaning 'large-chested'.

Bradyn

Gaelic, meaning 'descendant of Bradan'.

Bram

Gaelic, meaning 'raven'.

Brandon

Old English, meaning 'gorse'.

Brandt

Old English, meaning 'beacon'.

Brannon

Gaelic, meaning 'raven'.

Branson

English, meaning 'son of Brand'.

Brant

Old English, meaning 'hill'.

Braulio

Greek, meaning 'shining'.

Brendan

Gaelic, meaning 'prince'.

Brennan

Gaelic, meaning 'teardrop'.

Brenton

English, from Brent, meaning 'hill'.

Brett

English, meaning 'a brewer'.

Brewster

(alt. Brew, Brewer)

English, meaning 'a brewer'.

Brian

Gaelic, meaning 'high' or 'noble'.

Brice

Latin, meaning 'speckled'.

Brier

French, meaning 'heather'.

Brock

Old English, meaning 'badger'.

Broderick

English, meaning 'ruler'.

Brody

Gaelic, meaning both 'ditch' and 'brother'.

Brogan

Irish, meaning 'sturdy shoe'.

Bronwyn

Welsh, meaning 'white breasted'.

Brook

English, meaning 'stream'.

Bruce

Scottish, meaning 'high' or 'noble'.

Bruno

Germanic, meaning 'brown'.

Brutus

Latin, meaning 'dim-wit'. The name of Julius Caesar's assassin.

Bryant

English variant of Brian, meaning 'high' or 'noble'.

B

Bryce
Scottish, meaning 'of Britain'.

Brycen
Scottish, meaning 'son of Bryce'.

Bryden
Irish, meaning 'strong one'.

Bryson
Welsh, meaning 'descendant of Brice'.

Bubba
American, meaning 'boy'.

Buck
American, meaning 'goat' or 'deer'.

Bud
(alt. Buddy)
American, meaning 'friend'.

Burdett
Middle English, meaning 'bird'.

Burgess
(alt. Burges, Burgiss, Berje)
English, meaning 'business'.

Burke
French, meaning 'fortified settlement'.

Burl
French, meaning 'knotty wood'.

Buzz
American, shortened form of Busby, meaning 'village in the thicket'. Associated with the astronaut Buzz Aldrin.

Byron
Old English, meaning 'barn'. Made famous by the poet Lord Byron.

Sci-fi names

Anakin
Balin
Chike
Dante
Faizah
Fola
Hahzara
Kanene
Kibo
Shatea
Umi

C Boys' names

Cabot
Old English, meaning 'to sail'.

Cadby
(alt. Cadbey, Cadbee, Cadbie)
English, meaning 'soldier's colony'.

Cade
(alt. Caden)
English, meaning 'round, lumpy'.

Cadence
Latin, meaning 'with rhythm'.

Cadogan
Welsh, meaning 'battle glory and honour'.

Caedmon
Celtic, meaning 'wise warrior'.

Caelan
Gaelic, meaning 'slender'.

Caerwyn
(alt. Carwyn, Gerwyn)
Welsh, meaning 'white fort' or 'settlement'.

Caesar
Latin, meaning 'head of hair'. Made famous by the first Roman emperor Julius Caesar.

Caetano
Portuguese, meaning 'from Gaeta, Italy'.

Cagney
Irish, meaning 'successor of the advocate'.

C

Caiden
Arabic, meaning 'companion'.

Caillou
French, meaning 'pebble'.

Cain
Hebrew, meaning 'full of beauty'.

Cainan
Hebrew, meaning 'possessor' or 'purchaser'.

Cairo
Egyptian city.

Cal
Short form of names beginning Cal-.

Calder
Scottish, meaning 'rough waters'.

Caleb
Hebrew, meaning 'dog'.

Calen
From Caleb, meaning 'dog'.

Calhoun
Irish, meaning 'slight woods'.

Calix
Greek, meaning 'very handsome'.

Callahan
Irish, meaning 'contention' or 'strife'.

Callum
Gaelic, meaning 'dove'.

Calvin
French, meaning 'little bald one'.

Camden
Gaelic, meaning 'winding valley'. Also an area of north London.

Cameron
Scottish Gaelic, meaning 'crooked nose'.

Camillo
Latin, meaning 'free born' or 'noble'.

Campbell
Scottish Gaelic, meaning 'crooked mouth'.

C

Canaan
Hebrew, meaning 'to be humbled'.

Candido
Latin, meaning 'candid' or 'honest'.

Cannon
French, meaning 'of the church'.

Canton
French, meaning 'dweller of corner'. Also name given to areas of Switzerland.

Canute
(alt. Cnut, Cnute)
Scandinavian, meaning 'knot'. Name of the King of England in the 11th century.

Cappy
Italian, meaning 'lucky'.

Carden
Old English, meaning 'wool carder'.

Carey
Gaelic, meaning 'love'.

Carl
Old Norse, meaning 'free man'.

Carlo
Italian form of Carl, meaning 'free man'.

Carlos
Spanish form of Carl, meaning 'free man'.

Carlton
Old English, meaning 'free peasant settlement'.

Carmelo
Latin, meaning 'garden' or 'orchard'.

Carmen
Latin/Spanish, meaning 'song'.

Carmine
Latin, meaning 'song'.

Carnell
English, meaning 'defender of the castle'.

Carson
(alt. Carsten)
Scottish, meaning 'marsh-dwellers'.

Carter
Old English, meaning 'transporter of goods'.

C

Cary
Old Celtic river name. Also means 'love'.

Case
(alt. Casey)
Irish Gaelic, meaning 'alert' or 'watchful'.

Cash
Latin, shortened form of Cassius, meaning 'vain'.

Casimer
Slavic, meaning 'famous destroyer of peace'.

Cason
Latin, from Cassius, meaning 'empty' or 'hollow'.

Casper
Persian, meaning 'treasurer'.

Caspian
English, meaning 'of the Caspy people'. From the Caspian Sea.

Cassidy
Gaelic, meaning 'curly haired'.

Cassius
(alt. Cassio)
Latin, meaning 'empty, hollow'.

Cathal
Celtic, meaning 'battle rule'.

Cato
Latin, meaning 'all-knowing'.

TV personality names

Anthony (McPartlin)
Bill (Turnbull)
Bruce (Forsyth)
Declan (Donnelly)
Dermot (O'Leary)
Graham (Norton)
Keith (Lemon)
Louis (Walsh)
Phillip (Schofield)
Piers (Morgan)
Simon (Cowell)
Stephen (Fry)

Cecil
Latin, meaning 'blind'.

Cedar
English, from the name of an evergreen tree.

Cedric
Welsh, meaning 'spectacular bounty'.

Celestino
Spanish/Italian, meaning 'heavenly'.

Celesto
(alt. Celindo)
Latin, meaning 'heaven sent'.

Chad
(alt. Chadrick)
Old English, meaning 'warlike, warrior'.

Chaim
Hebrew, meaning 'life'.

Champion
English, from the word 'champion', meaning 'warrior'.

Chance
English, from the word 'chance' meaning 'good fortune'.

Chandler
Old English, meaning 'candle maker and seller'.

Charles
(alt. Charlie)
Old German, meaning 'free man'.

Chaska
Native American name usually given to first son.

Che
Spanish, shortened form of José. Made famous by Che Guevara.

Chesley
Old English, meaning 'camp on the meadow'.

Chester
Latin, meaning 'camp of soldiers'.

Chilton
(alt. Chillron, Chilly, Chilt)
English, meaning 'tranquil'.

Chima
Old English, meaning 'hilly land'.

Christian
English, from the word 'Christian'.

Christophe
French variant of Christopher, meaning 'bearing Christ inside'.

Christopher
Greek, meaning 'bearing Christ inside'.

Cian
Irish, meaning 'ancient'.

Ciaran
Irish, meaning 'black'.

Cicero
Latin, meaning 'chickpea'. Famous Roman philosopher and orator.

Cimarron
City in western Kansas.

Ciprian
Latin, meaning 'from Cyprus'.

Ciro
Spanish, meaning 'sun'.

Clancy
Old Irish, meaning 'red warrior'.

Clarence
Latin, meaning 'one who lives near the river Clare'.

Clark
Latin, meaning 'clerk'.

Claude
(alt. Claudie, Claudio, Claudius)
Latin, meaning 'lame'.

Claus
Variant of Nicholas, meaning 'people of victory'.

Clay
English, from the word 'clay'.

Clement
(alt. Clem)
Latin, meaning 'merciful'.

Cleo
Greek, meaning 'glory'.

C

Cletus
Greek, meaning 'illustrious'.

Cliff
(alt. Clifford, Clifton)
English, from the word 'cliff'.

Clint
(alt. Clinton)
Old English, meaning 'fenced settlement'.

Clive
Old English, meaning 'cliff' or 'slope'.

Clyde
Scottish, from the river in Glasgow.

Coby
(alt. Cody, Colby)
Irish, meaning 'son of Oda'.

Colden
Old English, meaning 'dark valley'.

Cole
Old French, meaning 'coal black'.

Coley
Old English, meaning 'coal black'.

Colin
Gaelic, meaning 'young creature'.

Colson
Old English, meaning 'coal black'.

Colton
English, meaning 'swarthy'.

Columbus
Latin, meaning 'dove'.

Colwyn
Welsh, from the river in Wales.

Conan
Gaelic, meaning 'wolf'.

Conley
Gaelic, meaning 'sensible'.

Connell
(alt. Connolly)
Irish, meaning 'high' or 'mighty'.

C

Connor
(alt. Conrad, Conroy)
Irish, meaning 'lover of hounds'.

Constant
(alt. Constantine)
English, from the word 'constant'.

Cooper
Old English, meaning 'barrel maker'.

Corban
Hebrew, meaning 'dedicated and belonging to God'.

Uncommon three-syllable names

Alastair
Barnaby
Dominic
Dorian
Elijah
Elliot
Lancelot
Roberto
Theodore

Corbett
(alt. Corbin, Corby)
Norman French, meaning 'young crow'.

Cordell
Old English, meaning 'cord maker'.

Corey
(alt. Cory)
Gaelic, meaning 'hill hollow'.

Corin
Latin, meaning 'spear'.

Corliss
(alt. Corlis, Corlyss, Corlys)
English, meaning 'benevolent'.

Cormac
Gaelic, meaning 'impure son'.

Cornelius
(alt. Cornell)
Latin, meaning 'horn'.

Cortez
Spanish, meaning 'courteous'.

C

Corwin
Old English, meaning 'heart's friend' or 'companion'.

Cosimo
(alt. Cosme, Cosmo)
Italian, meaning 'order' or 'beauty'.

Coty
French, meaning 'riverbank'.

Coulter
English, meaning 'young horse'.

Courtney
Old English, meaning 'domain of Curtis'.

Covey
English, meaning 'flock of birds'.

Cowan
Gaelic, meaning 'hollow in the hill'.

Craig
Welsh, meaning 'rock'.

Crispin
Latin, meaning 'curly haired'.

Croix
French, meaning 'cross'.

Cruz
Spanish, meaning 'cross'. Made famous by David and Victoria Beckham's son.

Cullen
Gaelic, meaning 'handsome'.

Curran
Gaelic, meaning 'dagger' or 'hero'.

Curtis
(alt. Curt)
Old French, meaning 'courteous'.

Cutler
Old English, meaning 'knife maker'.

Cyprian
English, meaning 'from Cyprus'.

Cyril
Greek, meaning 'master' or 'Lord'.

Cyrus
Persian, meaning 'Lord'.

C

Prime Ministers' names

Anthony (Eden, Blair)

Arthur (Wellesley, Balfour, Chamberlain)

David (Cameron)

Charles (Wentworth, Grey)

George (Grenville, Canning, Gordon)

Gordon (Brown)

Harold (Macmillan, Wilson)

Henry (Pelham, Fitzroy, Addington, Temple, Campbell-Bannerman, Asquith)

James (Balfour, MacDonald, Wilson)

John (Stuart, Russell, Major)

Margaret (Thatcher) for a girl

Robert (Walpole, Jenkinson, Peel, Gascoyne-Cecil)

Spencer (Crompton, Perceval)

William (Cavendish, Pitt (Elder and Younger), Wyndham, Lamb, Gladstone)

Boys' names

Dabeel
(alt. Dabee, Dabie, Daby)
Indian, meaning 'warrior'.

Dafydd
Welsh, meaning 'beloved'.
Made famous by the character
in the BBC TV series *Little
Britain*.

Daichi
Japanese, meaning 'great
wisdom'.

Daire
(alt. Daer, Daere, Dair)
Irish, meaning 'wealthy'.

Daisuke
Japanese, meaning
'lionhearted'.

Dakari
African, meaning 'happy'.

Dale
Old English, meaning 'valley'.

Dallin
English, meaning 'dweller in the
valley'.

Dalton
English, meaning 'town in the
valley'.

Daly
Gaelic, meaning 'assembly'.

Damarion
Greek, meaning 'gentle'.

D

Damian
(alt. Damon)
Greek, meaning 'to tame, subdue'.

Dane
Old English, meaning 'from Denmark'.

Daniel
(alt. Dan, Danny)
Hebrew, meaning 'God is my judge'.

Dante
Latin, meaning 'lasting'. Associated with the Italian 13th century poet Dante Alighieri author of *The Divine Comedy*.

Darby
Irish, meaning 'without envy'.

Darcy
Gaelic, meaning 'dark'. Associated with Jane Austen's Mr Darcy, and the parody of this character in *Bridget Jones' Diary*.

Dario
(alt. Darius)
Greek, meaning 'kingly'.

Darnell
Old English, meaning 'the hidden spot'.

Darragh
Irish, meaning 'dark oak'.

Darrell
(alt. Daryl)
Old English, meaning 'open'.

Darren
(alt. Darrian)
Gaelic, meaning 'great'.

Darrick
Old German, meaning 'power of the tribe'.

Darshan
Hindi, meaning 'vision'.

Darwin
Old English, meaning 'dear friend'. Often associated with the naturalist Charles Darwin.

Dash
(alt. Dashawn)
American, meaning 'enlightened one'.

D

Dashiell

French, meaning 'page boy'.

Dason

Native American, meaning 'chief'.

David

(alt. Dave, Davey, Davie, Davin)

Hebrew, meaning 'beloved'.

Davis

Old English, meaning 'son of David'.

Dawson

Old English, meaning 'son of David'.

Dax

(alt. Daxton)

French, once a town in south-western France. Now associated with the *Star Trek* character.

Dayal

Indian, meaning 'kind'.

Dayton

Old English, meaning 'David's place'.

Dean

Old English, meaning 'valley'.

Declan

Irish, meaning 'full of goodness'.

Dedric

Old English, meaning 'gifted ruler'.

Deepak

(alt. Deepan)

Indian, meaning 'illumination'.

Del

(alt. Delano, Delbert, Dell)

Old English, meaning 'bright shining one'.

Delaney

Irish, meaning 'dark challenge'.

Demetrius

Greek, meaning 'harvest lover'.

Dempsey

Irish, meaning 'proud'.

Denham

(alt. Denholm)

Old English, meaning 'valley settlement'.

D

Old name, new fashion?

Bertrand
Dexter
Felix
Hector
Jefferson
Norris
Pierce
Reginald
Ulysses
Winston

Dennis
(alt. Denny, Denton)
English, meaning 'follower of Dionysius'.

Denzil
(alt. Denzel)
English, meaning 'fort'. Also a town in Cornwall.

Deon
Greek, meaning 'of Zeus'.

Derek
English, meaning 'power of the tribe'.

Dermot
Irish, meaning 'free man'.

Desmond
Irish, meaning 'from south Munster'.

Destin
French, meaning 'destiny'.

Devyn
Irish, meaning 'poet'.

Dewey
Welsh, from Dewi (David).

Dexter
(alt. Dex)
Latin, meaning 'right-handed'.

Diallo
(alt. Dialo)
African, meaning 'bold'.

Dick
(alt. Dickie, Dickon)
From Richard, meaning 'powerful leader'.

Didier
French, meaning 'much desired'.

Diego
Spanish, meaning 'supplanter'.

Dietrich
Old German, meaning 'power of the tribe'.

Diggory
English, meaning 'dyke'.

Dilbert
English, meaning 'day-bright'.

Dimitri
(alt. Dimitrios, Dimitris)
Greek, meaning 'prince'.

Dino
Diminutive of Dean, meaning 'valley'.

Dion
Greek, short form of Dionysius, the Greek god of wine.

Dirk
Variant of Derek, meaning 'power of the tribe'.

Divakar
Sanskrit, meaning 'the sun'.

Dobbin
Diminutive of Robert, meaning 'bright fame'.

Dominic
Latin, meaning 'Lord'.

Donald
(alt. Don, Donal, Donaldo)
Gaelic, meaning 'great chief'.

Donato
Italian, meaning 'gift'.

Donnell
(alt. Donnie, Donny)
Gaelic, meaning 'world fighter'.

Donovan
Gaelic, meaning 'dark-haired chief'.

Doran
Gaelic, meaning 'exile'.

Dorian
Greek, meaning 'descendant of Doris'. Name of the title character in Oscar Wilde's *The Picture of Dorian Gray*.

D

Douglas
(alt. Dougal, Dougie)
Scottish, meaning 'black river'.

Doyle
Irish, meaning 'foreigner'.

Draco
Latin, meaning 'dragon'. Made popular by the character Draco Malfoy in the Harry Potter series.

Drake
Greek, meaning 'dragon'.

Drew
Shortened form of Andrew, Greek, meaning 'man' or 'warrior'.

Dryden
English, meaning 'dry town'.

Dudley
Old English, meaning 'people's field'. Also a town in the West Midlands, and the name of Harry Potter's cousin.

Duff
Gaelic, meaning 'swarthy'.

Duke
Latin, meaning 'leader'.

Duncan
Scottish, meaning 'dark warrior'.

Dustin
(alt. Dusty)
French, meaning 'brave warrior'.

Dwayne
Irish Gaelic, meaning 'swarthy'.

Dwight
Flemish, meaning 'blond'.

Dwyer
Gaelic, meaning 'dark wise one'.

Dyani
Native American, meaning 'eagle'.

Dylan
(alt. Dillon)
Welsh, meaning 'son of the sea'.

 Boys' names

Eagan
Irish, meaning 'fiery'.

Eamon
(alt. Eames)
Irish, meaning 'wealthy protector'.

Earl
(alt. Earle, Errol)
English, meaning 'nobleman, warrior, prince'.

Ebb
Shortened form of Ebenezer, meaning 'stone of help'.

Ebenezer
Hebrew, meaning 'stone of help'.

Ed
(alt. Edd, Eddie, Eddy)
Shortened form of Edward, meaning 'wealthy guard'.

Edgar
(alt. Elgar)
Old English, meaning 'wealthy spear'.

Edison
English, meaning 'son of Edward'.

Edmund
English, meaning 'wealthy protector'.

Edric
Old English, meaning 'rich and powerful'.

E

Edsel
Old German, meaning 'noble'.

Edward
(alt. Eduardo)
Old English, meaning 'wealthy guard'.

Edwin
English, meaning 'wealthy friend'.

Efrain
Hebrew, meaning 'fruitful'.

Egan
Irish, meaning 'fire'.

Eilif
(alt. Elif, Eilyg, Elyf)
Norse, meaning 'immortal'.

Einar
Old Norse, meaning 'battle leader'.

Eladio
Greek, meaning 'Greek'.

Elam
Hebrew, meaning 'eternal'.

Elbert
Old English, meaning 'famous'.

Eldon
Old English, meaning 'Ella's hill'.

Eldred
(alt. Eldridge)
Old English, meaning 'old venerable counsel'.

Elgin
Old English, meaning 'high minded'.

Eli
(alt. Eliah)
Hebrew, meaning 'high'.

Elias
(alt. Elijah)
Hebrew, meaning 'the Lord is my God'.

Elio
Spanish, meaning 'the Lord is my God'.

Ellery
Old English, meaning 'elder tree'.

Elliott
English variant of Elio, meaning 'the Lord is my God'.

Ellis
Welsh, variant of Elio, meaning 'the Lord is my God'.

Ellison

English, meaning 'son of Ellis'.

Elmer

(alt. Elmo)

Old English, meaning 'noble'; Arabic, meaning 'aristocratic'.

Elmo

(alt. Ellmo, Elmon)

Greek, meaning 'gregarious'. One of the characters in the children's TV series *Sesame Street*.

Elon

Hebrew, meaning 'oak tree'.

Elroy

French, meaning 'king'.

Elton

Old English, meaning 'Ella's town'.

Elvin

English, meaning 'elf-like'.

Elvis

Figure in Norse mythology. Made famous by the singer Elvis Presley.

Emanuel

Hebrew, meaning 'God is with us'.

Emeric

German, meaning 'work rule'.

Emile

(alt. Emiliano, Emilio)

Latin, meaning 'eager'.

Emlyn

Welsh, name of town, Newcastle Emlyn, in west Wales.

Emmett

English, meaning 'universal'.

Emrys

Welsh, meaning 'immortal'.

Eneco

Spanish, meaning 'fiery one'.

Enoch

Hebrew, meaning 'dedicated'.

Enrico

(alt. Enrique)

Italian, form of Henry, meaning 'home ruler'.

Enzo

Italian, short for Lorenzo, meaning 'laurel'.

117

E

Eoghan
(alt. Eoin)
Irish form of Owen, meaning 'well born' or 'noble'.

Eoin
Irish, meaning 'God is gracious'.

Ephron
(alt. Effron)
Hebrew, meaning 'dust'.

Erasmo
(alt. Erasmus)
Greek, meaning 'to love'.

Eric
Old Norse, meaning 'ruler'.

Ernest
(alt. Ernesto, Ernie, Ernst)
Old German, meaning 'serious'.

Errol
English, meaning 'boar wolf'.

Erskine
Scottish, meaning 'high cliff'. Also a place in Scotland.

Erwin
Old English, meaning 'boar friend'.

Eryx
Greek, meaning 'boxer'.

Ethan
(alt. Etienne)
Hebrew, meaning 'long lived'.

Eugene
Greek, meaning 'well born'.

Evan
Welsh, meaning 'God is good'.

Everard
Old English, meaning 'strong boar'.

Everett
English, meaning 'strong boar'.

Ewald
(alt. Ewan, Ewell)
Old English, from Owen, meaning 'well born' or 'noble'.

Exton
English, meaning 'on the River Exe'.

Ezra
Hebrew, meaning 'helper'. Associated with the poet Ezra Pound.

F

Boys' names

Faber
(alt. Fabir)
Latin, meaning 'blacksmith'.

Fabian
(alt. Fabien, Fabio)
Latin, meaning 'one who grows beans'.

Fabrice
(alt. Fabrizio)
Latin, meaning 'works with his hands'.

Faisal
Arabic, meaning 'resolute'.

Falco
(alt. Falcon, Falconer, Falke)
Latin, meaning 'falconer'.

Faron
Spanish, meaning 'pharaoh'.

Farrell
Gaelic, meaning 'hero'.

Faulkner
Latin, from 'falcon'.

Faustino
Latin, meaning 'fortunate'.

Fela
(alt. Felah, Fella, Fellah)
African, meaning 'a man who is warlike'. The name of the famous Nigerian musician Fela Kuti.

F

Names of poets

Andrew (Marvell)
Geoffrey (Chaucer)
Hugo (Williams)
John (Donne, Keats, Milton)
Percy (Bysshe Shelley)
Robert (Burns)
Siegfried (Sassoon)
Ted (Hughes)
Walt (Whitman)
William (Blake, Wordsworth)

Felipe
(alt. Filippo)
Spanish, meaning 'lover of horses'.

Felix
(alt. Felice)
Italian/Latin, meaning 'happy'.

Fennel
Latin, name of a herb.

Ferdinand
(alt. Fernando)
Old German, meaning 'bold voyager'.

Fergus
(alt. Ferguson)
Gaelic, meaning 'supreme man'.

Ferris
Gaelic, meaning 'rock'.

Fiachra
Irish, meaning 'raven'.

Fidel
Latin, meaning 'faithful'.

Finbar
Gaelic, meaning 'fair head'.

F

Finian

Gaelic, meaning 'fair'.

Finlay

(alt. Finley, Finn)

Gaelic, meaning 'fair haired courageous one'.

Finnegan

Gaelic, meaning 'fair'.

Fintan

Gaelic, meaning 'little fair one'.

Fitzroy

English, meaning 'the king's son'.

Flavio

Latin, meaning 'yellow hair'.

Florencio

(alt. Florentino)

Latin, meaning 'from Florence'.

Florian

(alt. Florin)

Slavic/Latin, meaning 'flower'.

Floyd

Welsh, meaning 'grey haired'.

Flynn

Gaelic, meaning 'with a ruddy complexion'.

Forbes

(alt. Forbs, Forb, Forbe)

Gaelic, meaning 'of the field'.

Fortunato

Italian, meaning 'lucky'.

Foster

Old English, meaning 'woodsman'.

Fotini

(alt. Fotis)

Greek, meaning 'light'.

Francesco

(alt. Francis, Francisco, Franco, François)

Latin, meaning 'from France'.

Frank

(alt. Frankie, Franklin, Franz)

Middle English, meaning 'free landholder'.

F

Fraser

Scottish, meaning 'of the forest men'.

Frederick

(alt. Freddie, Fred)

Old German, meaning 'peaceful ruler'.

Furman

Old German, meaning 'ferryman'.

Fyfe

(alt. Fife, Fyffes)

Scottish, meaning 'from Fifeshire'.

Boys' names

Gabe

Hebrew, shortened form of Gabriel, meaning 'hero of God'.

Gabino

Latin, meaning 'God is my strength'.

Gabriel

Hebrew, meaning 'hero of God'. One of the archangels.

Gael
(alt. Gale)

English, old reference to the Celts.

Gaius
(alt. Gaeus)

Latin, meaning 'rejoicing'.

Galen

Greek, meaning 'healer'.

Galileo

Italian, meaning 'from Galilee'.

Ganesh

Hindi, meaning 'Lord of the throngs'. One of the Hindu deities.

Gannon

Irish, meaning 'fair skinned'.

Gareth
(alt. Garth)

Welsh, meaning 'gentle'.

Garfield

Old English, meaning 'spear field'. Also the name of the cartoon cat.

G

Garland
English, as in 'garland of flowers'.

Garnet
English, precious stone, red in colour.

Garrett
Old German, meaning 'spear' or 'ruler'.

Garth
(alt. Garthe, Gart, Garte)
Norse, meaning 'enclosure'.

Gary
(alt. Garry, Geary)
Old English, meaning 'spear'.

Gaspar
(alt. Gaspard)
Persian, meaning 'treasurer'.

Gaston
From the Gascony region in the south of France.

Gavin
(alt. Gawain)
Scottish/Welsh, meaning 'little falcon'.

Gene
Greek, shortened form of Eugene, meaning 'well born'.

Genkei
Japanese, meaning 'honoured'.

Gennaro
Italian, meaning 'of Janus'.

Geoffrey
Old German, meaning 'peace'.

George
(alt. Giorgio)
Greek, meaning 'farmer'. Chosen by the Duke and Duchess of Cambridge for their son, born in July 2013.

Gerald
(alt. Geraldo, Gerard, Gerardo, Gerhard)
Old German, meaning 'spear ruler'.

Geronimo
Italian, meaning 'sacred name'.

Gerry
English, meaning 'independent'.

G

Gert
Old German, meaning 'strong spear'.

Gervase
Old German, meaning 'with honour'.

Giacomo
Italian, meaning 'God's son'.

Gibson
English, meaning 'son of Gilbert'.

Gideon
Hebrew, meaning 'tree cutter'.

Gilbert
(alt. Gilberto)
French, meaning 'bright promise'.

Giles
Greek, meaning 'small goat'.

Gino
Italian, meaning 'well born'.

Giovanni
Italian form of John, meaning 'God is gracious'.

Giri
(alt. Gririe, Giry, Girey)
Indian, meaning 'from the mountain'.

Giulio
Italian, meaning 'youthful'.

Giuseppe
Italian form of Joseph, meaning 'Jehovah increases'.

Glen
English, from the word 'glen'.

Glyn
Welsh form of Glen.

Godfrey
German, meaning 'peace of God'.

Gordon
Gaelic, meaning 'large fortification'.

Gottlieb
German, meaning 'good love'.

Gower
Area on the Welsh coast.

G

Graeme
(alt. Graham)
English, meaning 'gravelled area'.

Grant
English, from the word 'grant'.

Granville
English, meaning 'gravelly town'.

Gray
(alt. Grey)
English, from the word 'gray'.

Grayson
English, meaning 'son of gray'.

Green
English, from the word 'green'.

Greg
(alt. Gregorio, Gregory, Grieg)
English, meaning 'watcher'.

Griffin
English, from the word 'griffin'.

Groves
English, meaning 'inhabits near grove of trees'.

Grylfi
(alt. Gylfie, Gylfee, Gylffi)
Scandinavian, meaning 'king'.

Guido
Italian, meaning 'guide'.

Guillaume
French form of William, meaning 'strong protector'.

Gulliver
English, meaning 'glutton'.

Gunther
German, meaning 'warrior'.

Gurpreet
Indian, meaning 'love of the teacher'.

Gustave
(alt. Gus)
Scandinavian, meaning 'royal staff'.

Guy
English, from the word 'guy'.

Gwyn
Welsh, meaning 'white'.

 Boys' names

 H

Habib
Arabic, meaning 'beloved one'.

Hackett
(alt. Hacket, Hackit, Hackitt)
German, meaning 'small hacker'.

Haden
(alt. Haiden)
English, meaning 'hedged valley'.

Hades
Greek, meaning 'sightless'. Name of the underworld in Greek mythology.

Hadrian
From Hadria, a north Italian city.

Hadwin
Old English, meaning 'friend in war'.

Hakeem
Arabic, meaning 'wise and insightful'.

Hal
(alt. Hale, Hallie)
English, nickname for Henry, meaning 'home ruler'.

Halim
Arabic, meaning 'gentle'.

Hallam
Old English, meaning 'the valley'.

Hamid
Arabic, meaning 'praiseworthy'.

127

H

Hamilton

Old English, meaning 'flat topped hill'.

Hamish

Scottish form of James, meaning 'he who supplants'.

Hamlet

(alt. Hamlett, Hammet, Hamnet)

German, meaning 'village'. A variation of the Danish Amleth, and often associated with Shakespeare's tragedy *Hamlet*.

Hampus

Swedish form of Homer, meaning 'pledge'.

Hamza

Arabic, meaning 'lamb'.

Han

(alt. Hannes, Hans)

Scandinavian, meaning 'the Lord is gracious'.

Hanif

(alt. Haneef, Haneaf, Haneif)

Arabic, meaning 'devout'.

Hank

German, form of Henry, meaning 'home ruler'.

Hansel

German, meaning 'the Lord is gracious'.

Hardy

English, meaning 'tough'. Often associated with the author Thomas Hardy.

Harlan

English, meaning 'dweller by the boundary wood'.

Names from ancient Greece

Aeschylus
Erasmus
Hieronymus
Homer
Jason
Leonidas
Nikolaos
Sophocles
Theodore

Harland

Old English, meaning 'army land'.

Harley

Old English, meaning 'hare meadow'.

Harmon

Old German, meaning 'soldier'.

Harold

Scandinavian, meaning 'army ruler'.

Harry

Old German, form of Henry, meaning 'home ruler'.

Hart

Old English, meaning 'stag'.

Harvey

Old English, meaning 'strong and worthy'.

Haskell

Hebrew, meaning 'intellect'.

Hassan

Arabic, meaning 'handsome'.

Haydn

(alt. Hayden, Haydon)

Old English, meaning 'hedged valley'.

Heart

English, from the word 'heart'.

Heath

English, meaning 'heath' or 'moor'.

Heathcliff

English, meaning 'cliff near a heath'. Made famous by Emily Bronte's novel *Wuthering Heights*.

Heber

Hebrew, meaning 'partner'.

Hector

Greek, meaning 'steadfast'.

Henry

(alt. Henri, Hendrik, Hendrix)

Old German, meaning 'home ruler'.

Henson

English, meaning 'son of Henry'.

Herbert
(alt. Bert, Herb)
Old German, meaning 'illustrious warrior'.

Heriberto
Spanish variant of Herbert, meaning 'illustrious warrior'.

Herman
(alt. Herminio, Hermon)
Old German, meaning 'soldier'.

Hermes
Greek, meaning 'messenger'. The messenger of the gods in Greek mythology.

Herschel
Yiddish, meaning 'deer'.

Hezekiah
Hebrew, meaning 'God gives strength'.

Hideki
Japanese, meaning 'excellent trees'.

Hideo
Japanese, meaning 'excellent name'.

Hilario
Latin, meaning 'cheerful, happy'.

Hilary
English, meaning 'cheerful'.

Hillel
Hebrew, meaning 'greatly praised'.

Hilliard
Old German, meaning 'battle guard'.

Hilton
Old English, meaning 'hill settlement'.

Hiram
Hebrew, meaning 'exalted brother'.

Hiro
Spanish, meaning 'sacred name'.

Hiroshi
Japanese, meaning 'generous'.

Hirsch
Yiddish, meaning 'deer'.

H

Hobart

English, meaning 'bright and shining intellect'.

Hodge

English, meaning 'son of Roger'.

Hogan

Gaelic, meaning 'youth'.

Holden

English, meaning 'deep valley'.

Hollis

Old English, meaning 'holly tree'.

Homer

Greek, meaning 'pledge'. Name of the Greek poet, and the TV character Homer Simpson.

Honorius

Latin, meaning 'honourable'.

Horace

Latin, name of the Roman poet.

Houston

Old English, meaning 'Hugh's town'. Also a city in the state of Texas, US.

Howard

Old English, meaning 'noble watchman'.

Howell

Welsh, meaning 'eminent and remarkable'.

Hoyt

Norse, meaning 'spirit' or 'soul'.

Hristo

From Christo, meaning 'follower of Christ'.

Hubbell
(alt. Hubble)

English, meaning 'brave hearted'.

Hubert

German, meaning 'bright and shining intellect'.

Hudson

Old English, meaning 'son of Hugh'.

Hugh

Old German, meaning 'soul, mind and intellect'.

H

Hugo

German, meaning 'bright in mind and spirit'.

Humbert

Old German, meaning 'famous giant'. Be warned: it's the name and surname of the paedophile protagonist of Vladimir Nabokov's *Lolita*.

Humphrey

Old German, meaning 'peaceful warrior'.

Hunter

English, from the word 'hunter'.

Hurley

Gaelic, meaning 'sea tide'.

Huxley

Old English, meaning 'Hugh's meadow'.

Hyrum

Hebrew, meaning 'exalted brother'.

Surnames as first names

Cameron	Jackson
Campbell	Lewis
Connor	Mason
Cooper	Taylor
Hamilton	Walker
Harrison	Watson

I Boys' names

Iago
Spanish, meaning 'he who supplants'. Name of the villain in Shakespeare's *Othello*.

Ian
(alt. Ion)
Gaelic, variant of John, meaning 'God is gracious'.

Ianto
Welsh, meaning 'gift of God'.

Ibaad
Arabic, meaning 'a believer in God'.

Ibrahim
Arabic, meaning 'father of many'.

Ichabod
Hebrew, meaning 'glory is good'.

Ichiro
Japanese, meaning 'firstborn son'.

Idan
Hebrew, meaning 'place in time'.

Idris
Welsh, meaning 'fiery leader'.

Ifan
Welsh variant of John, meaning 'God is gracious'.

I

Ignacio
Latin, meaning 'ardent' or 'burning'.

Ignatz
German, meaning 'fiery'.

Igor
Russian, meaning 'Ing's soldier'.

Ikaika
Hawaiian, meaning 'strong'.

Ike
Hebrew, short for Isaac, meaning 'laughter'.

Iku
Japanese, meaning 'nourishing'.

Ilan
Hebrew, meaning 'tree'.

Ilias
Variant of Hebrew Elijah, meaning 'the Lord is my God'.

Imanol
Hebrew, meaning 'God is with us'.

Indiana
Latin, meaning 'from India'. Also a state in the US.

Indigo
English, describing a deep blue colour.

Indio
Spanish, meaning 'indigenous people'.

Ingo
Danish, meaning 'meadow'.

Inigo
Spanish, meaning 'fiery'.

Girls' names for boys (male spellings)

Darcy
Gene (or Jean in France)
Kay
Kelly
Kelsey
Madison
Nat
Paris
Sandy
Sasha

Ioannis

Greek, meaning 'the Lord is gracious'.

Iovianno

Native American, meaning 'yellow hawk'.

Ira

Hebrew, meaning 'full grown and watchful'.

Irvin
(alt. Irving, Irwin)

Gaelic, meaning 'green and fresh water'.

Isaac
(alt. Isaak)

Hebrew, meaning 'laughter'.

Isadore
(alt. Isidore, Isidro)

Greek, meaning 'gift of Isis'.

Isai
(alt. Isaiah, Isaias, Izaiah)

Arabic, meaning 'protection and security'.

Iser

Yiddish, meaning 'God wrestler'.

Place names

Austin
Carson
Chester
Glen
Jericho
London
Paris
Seymour
Tennessee
Whitley
Windsor

Ishedus

Native American, meaning 'on top'.

Ishmael
(alt. Ismael)

Hebrew, meaning 'God listens'.

Israel

Hebrew, meaning 'God perseveres'. Also the name of the country.

Istvan

Hungarian variant of Stephen, meaning 'crowned'.

Itai

Hebrew, meaning 'the Lord is with me'.

135

I

Ivan

Hebrew, meaning 'God is gracious'.

Ivanhoe

Russian, meaning 'God is gracious'. Also name of the novel by Walter Scott.

Ivey

English, variant of Ivy.

Ivo

French, from the word 'yves', meaning 'yew tree'.

Ivor

Scandinavian, meaning 'yew'.

Ivory

English, from the word 'ivory'.

Izar

Basque, meaning 'star'.

J Boys' names

Jabari
Swahili, meaning 'valiant'.

Jabez
Hebrew, meaning 'borne in pain'.

Jabulani
(alt. Jabulanie, Jabulany, Jabulaney)
African, meaning 'happy one'.

Jace
(alt. Jaece, Jase, Jayce)
Hebrew, meaning 'healer'.

Jacek
African, meaning 'hyacinth'.

Jacinto
African, meaning 'hyacinth'.

Jack
(alt. Jackie, Jacky) ·
From the Hebrew John, meaning 'God is gracious'. The UK's most popular boy's name for 14 years until 2011.

Jackson
English, meaning 'son of Jack'.

Jaco
Hebrew, from Jacob, meaning 'he who supplants'.

Jacob
(alt. Jacobo, Jago)
Hebrew, meaning 'he who supplants'.

Jacques
French form of Jack, meaning 'God is gracious'.

J

Jaden
*(alt. Jaden, Jadyn, Jaeden,
Jaiden, Jaidyn, Jayden, Jaydin)*
Hebrew, meaning 'Jehovah has
heard'.

Jaegar
(alt. Jager, Jaecer, Jaegar)
German, meaning 'mighty
hunter'.

Jafar
Arabic, meaning 'stream'.

Jagger
Old English, meaning 'one who
cuts'.

Jaheem
(alt. Jaheim)
Hebrew, meaning 'raised up'.

Jahir
Hindi, meaning 'jewel'.

Jaime
Variant of James, meaning
'he who supplants'. 'J'aime' is
French for 'I love'.

Jair
(alt. Jairo)
Hebrew, meaning 'God
enlightens'.

Jake
Shortened form of Jacob,
meaning 'he who supplants'.

Jalen
Greek, meaning 'healer' or
'tranquil'.

Jali
Swahili, meaning 'musician'.

Jalon
Greek, meaning 'healer' or
'tranquil'.

Jamaal
(alt. Jamal)
Arabic, meaning 'handsome'.

Jamar
*(alt. Jamarcus, Jamari, Jamarion,
Jamir)*
Modern variant of Jamaal,
meaning 'handsome'.

Jamel
Arabic, meaning 'handsome'.

J

James
English, meaning 'he who supplants'.

Jameson
(alt. Jamison)
English, meaning 'son of James'.

Jamie
(alt. Jamey, Jaimie)
Nickname for James, meaning 'he who supplants'.

Jamil
Arabic, meaning 'handsome'.

Short names

Al
Ben
Dev
Ed
Jo
Kev
Max
Rob
Sam
Ty

Jamin
Hebrew, meaning 'son of the right hand'.

Jan
(alt. Janko, János)
Slavic, from John, meaning 'the Lord is gracious'.

Janesh
Hindi, meaning 'leader of people'.

Janus
Latin, meaning 'gateway'. Roman god of doors, beginnings and endings.

Japhet
(alt. Japheth)
Hebrew, meaning 'comely'.

Jaquez
French, form of Jacques, meaning 'God is gracious'.

Jared
(alt. Jarem, Jaren, Jaret, Jarod, Jarrod)
Hebrew, meaning 'descending'.

J

Jarlath
Gaelic, from Iarlaith, from Saint Iarfhlaith.

Jarom
Greek, meaning 'to raise and exalt'.

Jarrell
Variant of Gerald, meaning 'spear ruler'.

Jarrett
Old English, meaning 'spear-brave'.

Jarvis
Old German, meaning 'with honour'.

Jason
Greek, meaning 'healer'.

Jasper
Greek, meaning 'treasure holder'.

Javen
Arabic, meaning 'youth'.

Javier
Spanish, meaning 'bright'.

Jaxon
From Jackson, meaning 'son of Jack'.

Jay
Latin, meaning 'jaybird'.

Jaylan
Greek, meaning 'healer'.

Jeevan
Indian, meaning 'life'.

Jefferson
English, meaning 'son of Jeffrey'.

Jeffrey
(alt. Jeff)
Old German, meaning 'peace'.

Jensen
Scandinavian, meaning 'son of Jan'.

Jeremiah
(alt. Jeremia, Jeremias, Jeremiya)
Hebrew, meaning 'the Lord exalts'.

J

Jeremy
(alt. Jem)

Hebrew, meaning 'the Lord exalts'.

Jeriah

Hebrew, meaning 'Jehovah has seen'.

Jericho

Arabic, meaning 'city of the moon'.

Jermaine

Latin, meaning 'brotherly'.

Jerome

Greek, meaning 'sacred name'.

Jerry

English, from Gerald, meaning 'spear ruler'.

Jesse

Hebrew, meaning 'the Lord exists'.

Jesus

Hebrew, meaning 'the Lord is Salvation' and the Son of God.

Jet
(alt. Jelt)

English, meaning 'black gemstone'.

Jethro

Hebrew, meaning 'eminent'.

Jim
(alt. Jimmy)

From James, meaning 'he who supplants'.

Jiri
(alt. Jiro)

Greek, meaning 'farmer'.

Joachim

Hebrew, meaning 'established by God'.

Joah
(alt. João)

Hebrew, meaning 'God is gracious'.

Joaquin

Hebrew, meaning 'established by God'. Made famous by the actor Joaquin Phoenix.

J

Joe
(alt. Joey, Johan, Johannes, Jomar)
From Joseph, meaning 'Jehovah increases'.

Joel
Hebrew, meaning 'Jehovah is the Lord'.

John
Hebrew, meaning 'God is gracious'.

Johnny
(alt. Jon, Jonny)
From Jonathan, meaning 'gift of God'.

Jolyon
From Julian, meaning 'young'.

Jonah
Hebrew, meaning 'dove'.

Jonas
Hebrew, meaning 'dove'.

Jonathan
(alt. Johnathan, Johnathon, Jonathon, Jonty)
Hebrew, meaning 'God is gracious'.

Jordan
(alt. Jory, Judd)
Hebrew, meaning 'down-flowing'.

Jorge
From George, meaning 'farmer'.

José
Spanish variant of Joseph, meaning 'God increases'.

Joseph
(alt. Joss)
Hebrew, meaning 'God increases'.

Josh
Shortened form of Joshua, meaning 'God is salvation'.

Joshua
Hebrew, meaning 'God is salvation'.

Josiah
Hebrew, meaning 'God helps'.

Josué
Spanish variant of Joshua, meaning 'God is salvation'.

J

'Bad boy' names

Arnie
Axel
Brett
Conan
Damian
Guy
Ivan
Preston
Stanley
Tyson

Jovan

Latin, meaning 'the supreme God'.

Joweese

Native American, meaning 'chirping bird'.

Joyce

Latin, meaning 'joy'.

Juan

Spanish variant of John, meaning 'God is gracious'.

Jubal

Hebrew, meaning 'ram's horn'.

Jude

Hebrew, meaning 'praise' or 'thanks'. The title character in Hardy's novel *Jude the Obscure*.

Judson

Variant of Jude, meaning 'praise' or 'thanks'.

Jules

From Julian, meaning 'Jove's child'.

Julian

Greek, meaning 'Jove's child'.

Julien

French variant of Julian, meaning 'Jove's child'.

Julio

Spanish variant of Julian, meaning 'Jove's child'.

Julius

Latin, meaning 'youthful'.

Junior

Latin, meaning 'the younger one'.

J

Junius

Latin, meaning 'young'.

Jupiter

Latin, meaning 'the supreme God'. Jupiter was king of the Roman gods and the god of thunder. Jupiter is also the largest planet in the solar system.

Juraj

Hebrew, meaning 'God is my judge'.

Jurgen

Greek, meaning 'farmer'.

Justice

English, from the word 'justice'.

Justin

(alt. Justus)

Latin, meaning 'just and upright'.

Juwan

Hebrew, meaning 'the Lord is gracious'.

Famous male drummers

Dave (Grohl)
John (Bonham)
Keith (Moon)
Lars (Ulrich)
Mick (Fleetwood)

Phil (Collins)
Ringo (Starr)
Stewart (Copeland)
Tommy (Lee)
Travis (Barker)

K

Boys' names

Kaamil

Arabic, meaning 'perfect'.

Kabelo

African, meaning 'gift'.

Kade

Scottish, meaning 'from the wetlands'.

Kadeem

Arabic, meaning 'one who serves'.

Kaden

(alt. *Kadin, Kaeden, Kaedin, Kaiden)*

Arabic, meaning 'companion'.

Kadir

Arabic, meaning 'capable and competent'.

Kafka

Czech, meaning 'bird-like'. Often associated with the author of *The Metamorphosis*.

Kahekili

Hawaiian, meaning 'the thunder'.

Kahlil

Arabic, meaning 'friend'.

Kai

Greek, meaning 'keeper of the keys'.

Kaito

Japanese, meaning 'ocean and sake dipper'.

Kalani

Hawaiian, meaning 'sky'.

Kale

German, meaning 'free man'.

Kaleb
(alt. Caleb)

Hebrew, meaning 'dog' or 'aggressive'.

Kalen

Gaelic, meaning 'uncertain'.

Kaleo

Hawaiian, meaning 'the voice'.

Kalil

Arabic, meaning 'friend'.

Kalvin

French, meaning 'bald'.

Kamari

Indian, meaning 'the enemy of desire'.

Kamden

English, meaning 'winding valley'.

Kamil

Arabic, meaning 'perfection'.

Kane

Gaelic, meaning 'little battler'.

Kani

Hawaiian, meaning 'sound'.

Kanye

African town. Made popular by rapper Kanye West.

Kareem
(alt. Karim)

Arabic, meaning 'generous'.

Karl
(alt. Karson)

Old German, meaning 'free man'.

Kasey

Irish, meaning 'alert'.

Kaspar

Persian, meaning 'treasurer'.

Kavon

Gaelic, meaning 'handsome'.

Kayden

Arabic, meaning 'companion'.

Kazimierz

Polish, meaning 'declares peace'.

Kazuki

Japanese, meaning 'radiant hope'.

Kazuo

Japanese, meaning 'harmonious man'.

Keagan
(alt. Keegan, Kegan)

Gaelic, meaning 'small flame'.

Keane

Gaelic, meaning 'fighter'.

Keanu

Hawaiian, meaning 'breeze'. Made famous by the actor Keanu Reeves.

Keary

Gaelic, meaning 'black-haired'.

Keaton

English, meaning 'place of hawks'.

Keefe
(alt. Keef, Kief, Kiefe)

Gaelic, meaning 'beautiful and graceful'.

Keeler

Gaelic, meaning 'beautiful and graceful'.

Keenan
(alt. Kenan)

Gaelic, meaning 'little ancient one'.

Keiji

Japanese, meaning 'govern with discretion'.

Keir

Gaelic, meaning 'dark-haired' or 'dark-skinned'.

Keith

Gaelic, meaning 'woodland'.

Kekoa

Hawaiian, meaning 'brave one' or 'soldier'.

Kelby

Old English, meaning 'farmhouse near the stream'.

K

Kell
(alt. Kellan, Kellen, Kelley, Kelly, Kiel)
Norse, meaning 'spring'.

Kelsey
Old English, meaning 'victorious ship'.

Kelton
Old English, meaning 'town of the keels'.

Kelvin
Old English, meaning 'friend of ships'.

Kemenes
Hungarian, meaning 'maker of furnaces'.

Ken
Shortened form of Kenneth, meaning 'born of fire'.

Kendal
Old English, meaning 'the Kent river valley'.

Kendon
Old English, meaning 'brave guard'.

Kendrick
Gaelic, meaning 'royal ruler'.

Kenelm
Old English, meaning 'bold'.

Kenji
Japanese, meaning 'intelligent second son'.

Kennedy
Gaelic, meaning 'helmet head'.

Kenneth
(alt. Kenney)
Gaelic, meaning 'born of fire'.

Kennison
English, meaning 'son of Kenneth'.

Kent
From the English county.

Kenton
English, meaning 'town of Ken'.

Kenya
From the country in Africa.

Kenzo
Japanese, meaning 'wise'.

K

Keola
Hawaiian, meaning 'life'.

Keon
(alt. Kean, Keoni)
Hawaiian, meaning 'gracious'.

Kepler
German, meaning 'hat maker'.

Kermit
(alt. Kerwin)
Gaelic, meaning 'without envy'. Associated with Kermit the Frog, the Muppets character.

Kerr
English, meaning 'wetland'.

Keshav
Indian, meaning 'beautiful-haired'.

Kevin
Gaelic, meaning 'handsome beloved'.

Khalid
(alt. Khalif, Khalil)
Arabic, meaning 'immortal'.

Kian
(alt. Keyon, Kyan)
Irish, meaning 'ancient'.

Kiefer
German, meaning 'barrel maker'.

Literary names

Charlie (*Charlie and the Chocolate Factory*, Roald Dahl)
Christopher (*Now We Are Six*, A. A. Milne)
Gabriel (*Far from the Madding Crowd*, Thomas Hardy)
Dorian (*The Picture of Dorian Gray*, Oscar Wilde)
Ishmael (*Moby Dick*, Herman Melville)
James (*James and the Giant Peach*, Roald Dahl)
Karin (*The Buddha of Suburbia*, Hanif Kureishi)
Peeta (*The Hunger Games*, Suzanne Collins)
Phileas (*Around the World in Eighty Days*, Jules Verne)
Richard (*The Beach*, Alex Garland)
Winston (*Nineteen Eighty-Four*, George Orwell)

K

Kieran
(alt. Kyron)
Gaelic, meaning 'black'.

Kijana
African, meaning 'youth'.

Kilby
From the English 'Cilebi', a place in Leicestershire.

Kilian
Irish, meaning 'bright headed'.

Kimani
African, meaning 'beautiful and sweet'.

King
English, from the word 'king'.

Kingsley
English, meaning 'the king's meadow'.

Kirby
German, meaning 'settlement by a church'.

Kirk
Old German, meaning 'church'.

Klaus
German, meaning 'victorious'.

Knightley
(alt. Knightly)
English, meaning 'of the knight's meadows'. Surname of the hero in Jane Austen's *Emma*.

Kobe
(alt. Koda, Kody)
Japanese, meaning 'a Japanese city'.

Kofi
Ghanaian, meaning 'born on Friday'.

Kohana
Japanese, meaning 'little flower'.

Kojo
Ghanaian, meaning 'Monday'.

Kolby
Norse, meaning 'settlement'.

Korbin
Gaelic, meaning 'a steep hill'.

Kramer

German, meaning 'shopkeeper'.

Kris

(alt. Krish)

From Christopher, meaning 'bearing Christ inside'.

Kurt

German, meaning 'courageous advice'.

Kurtis

French, meaning 'courtier'.

Kwame

Ghanaian, meaning 'born on Saturday'.

Kyden

English, meaning 'narrow little fire'.

Kylan

(alt. Kyle, Kyleb, Kyler)

Gaelic, meaning 'narrow and straight'.

Kyllion

Irish, meaning 'war'.

Kyree

From Cree, a Canadian tribe.

Kyros

Greek, meaning 'legitimate power'.

English and Scottish royalty

Alexander	James
Charles	Richard
Edward	Robert
George	Stephen
Henry	William

L Boys' names

Laban
Hebrew, meaning 'white'.

Lachlan
Gaelic, meaning 'from the land of lakes'.

Lacy
Old French, after the place in France.

Laertes
English, meaning 'adventurous'. Ophelia's brother in Shakespeare's *Hamlet*.

Lalit
Hindi, meaning 'beautiful'.

Lamar
Old German, meaning 'water'.

Lambert
Scandinavian, meaning 'land brilliant'.

Lambros
Greek, meaning 'brilliant and radiant'.

Lamont
Old Norse, meaning 'law man'.

Lance
French, meaning 'land'.

Lancelot
Variant of Lance, meaning 'land'. The name of one of the Knights of the Round Table.

Landen
(*alt. Lando, Landon, Langdon*)
English, meaning 'long hill'.

L

Landyn
Welsh variant of Landen, meaning 'long hill'.

Lane
(alt. Layne)
English, from the word 'lanel'.

Lang
Norse, meaning 'long meadow'.

Lannie
(alt. Lanny)
German, meaning 'precious'.

Larkin
Gaelic, meaning 'rough' or 'fierce'.

Laron
French, meaning 'thief'.

Larry
Latin, variant of Lawrence, meaning 'man from Laurentum'.

Lars
Scandinavian variant of Lawrence, meaning 'man from Laurentum'.

Lasse
Finnish, meaning 'girl'. (Still, ironically, a boy's name.)

Laszlo
Hungarian, meaning 'glorious rule'.

Lathyn
Latin, meaning 'fighter'.

Latif
Arabic, meaning 'gentle'.

Laurel
Latin, meaning 'bay'.

Laurent
French form of Lawrence, meaning 'man from Laurentum'.

Lawrence
Latin, meaning 'man from Laurentum'.

Lazarus
Hebrew, meaning 'God is my help'.

Leandro
Latin, meaning 'lion man'.

Lear
German, meaning 'of the meadow'.

Lee
(alt. Leigh)
Old English, meaning 'meadow' or 'valley'.

Leib
German, meaning 'love'.

Leif
Scandinavian, meaning 'heir'.

Leith
From the name of a place in Scotland.

Lennox
(alt. Lenny)
Gaelic, meaning 'with many elm trees'.

Leo
Latin, meaning 'lion'.

Leon
Latin, meaning 'lion'.

Leonard
Old German, meaning 'lion strength'.

Leopold
German, meaning 'brave people'.

Leroy
French, meaning 'king'.

Lesley
(alt. Les)
Scottish, meaning 'holly garden'.

Lester
English, meaning 'from Leicester'.

Lewis
French, meaning 'renowned fighter'.

Lex
English variant of Alexander, meaning 'defending men'.

Liam
German, meaning 'helmet'.

Lincoln
English, meaning 'lake colony'.

L

Lindsay
Scottish, meaning 'linden tree'.

Linus
Latin, meaning 'lion'.

Lionel
English, meaning 'lion'.

Llewellyn
Welsh, meaning 'like a lion'.

Lloyd
Welsh, meaning 'grey-haired and sacred'.

Logan
Gaelic, meaning 'hollow'.

Lonnie
English, meaning 'lion strength'.

Lorcan
Gaelic, meaning 'little fierce one'.

Louis
(alt. Lou, Louie, Luigi, Luis)
German, meaning 'famous warrior'.

Lucas
(alt. Lukas, Luca)
English, meaning 'man from Luciana'.

Lucian
(alt. Lucio)
Latin, meaning 'light'.

Ludwig
German, meaning 'famous fighter'.

Luke
(alt. Luc, Luka)
Latin, meaning 'from Lucanus'.

Lupe
Latin, meaning 'wolf'.

Luther
German, meaning 'soldier of the people'.

Lyle
French, meaning 'the island'.

Lyn
(alt. Lyndon)
Spanish, meaning 'pretty'.

Boys' names

Mabon
(alt. Maban, Mabery)
Welsh, meaning 'our son'.

Mac
(alt. Mack, Mackie)
Scottish, meaning 'son of'.

Macaulay
Scottish, meaning 'son of the phantom'.

Mace
English, meaning 'heavy staff' or 'club'.

Mackenzie
Scottish, meaning 'the fair one'.

Mackland
Scottish, meaning 'land of Mac'.

Macon
French, name of towns in France and Georgia.

Macsen
Scottish, meaning 'son of Mac'.

Madden
Irish, meaning 'descendant of the hound'.

Maddox
English, meaning 'good' or 'generous'.

Madison
(alt. Madsen)
Irish, meaning 'son of Madden'.

Mads
Shortened form of Madden, meaning 'descendant of the hound'.

Magnus
(alt. Manus)
Latin, meaning 'great'.

Maguire
Gaelic, meaning 'son of the beige one'.

Mahabala
Indian, meaning 'great strength'.

Mahesh
Hindi, meaning 'great ruler'.

Mahir
Arabic, meaning 'skilful'.

Mahlon
Hebrew, meaning 'sickness'.

Mahmoud
Arabic, meaning 'praiseworthy'.

Mahoney
Irish, meaning 'bear'.

Major
English, from the word 'major'.

Makal
From Michael, meaning 'close to God'.

Makani
Hawaiian, meaning 'wind'.

Makis
Hebrew, meaning 'gift from God'.

Mako
Hebrew, meaning 'God is with us'.

Malachi
(alt. Malachy)
Irish, meaning 'messenger of God'.

Malcolm
English, meaning 'Columba's servant'.

Mali
Arabic, meaning 'full and rich'.

Manfred
Old German, meaning 'man of peace'.

Manish

English, meaning 'manly'.

Manley

English, meaning 'manly and brave'.

Mannix

Gaelic, meaning 'little monk'.

Manoi
(alt. Manos)

Japanese, meaning 'love springing from intellect'.

Manuel

Hebrew, meaning 'God is with us'.

Manzi

Italian, meaning 'steer'.

Marc
(alt. Marco, Marcos, Marcus, Markel)

French, meaning 'from the god Mars'.

Marcel
(alt. Marcelino, Marcello)

French, meaning 'little warrior'.

Marek

Polish variant of Mark, meaning 'from the god Mars'.

Mariano

Latin, meaning 'from the god Mars'.

Mario
(alt. Marius)

Latin, meaning 'manly'.

Mark
(alt. Markus)

English, meaning 'from the god Mars'.

Marley
(alt. Marlin)

Old English, meaning 'meadow near the lake'.

Marlon

English, meaning 'like little hawk'.

Marshall

Old French, meaning 'caretaker of horses'.

Martin

Latin, meaning 'dedicated to Mars'.

Marty

Shortened form of Martin, meaning 'dedicated to Mars'.

Marvel

English, from the word 'marvel'.

Marvin

Welsh, meaning 'sea friend'.

Mason

English, from the word 'mason'.

Massimo

Italian, meaning 'greatest'.

Mathias
(alt. Matthias)

Hebrew, meaning 'gift of the Lord'.

Mathieu

French form of Matthew, meaning 'gift of God'.

Matthew

Hebrew, meaning 'gift of the Lord'.

Maurice
(alt. Mauricio)

Latin, meaning 'dark skinned' or 'Moorish'.

Maverick

American, meaning 'non-conformist leader'.

Max
(alt. Maxie, Maxim)

Latin, meaning 'greatest'.

Maximillian

Latin, meaning 'greatest'.

Maximino

Latin, meaning 'little Max'.

Maxwell

Latin, meaning 'Maccus' stream'.

Maynard

Old German, meaning 'brave'.

McArthur

Scottish, meaning 'son of Arthur'.

McCoy

Scottish, meaning 'son of Coy'.

Mearl

English, meaning 'my earl'.

Mederic
French, meaning 'doctor'.

Mekhi
African, meaning 'who is God?'.

Mel
Gaelic, meaning 'smooth brow'.

Melbourne
From the city in Australia.

Melchior
Persian, meaning 'king of the city'.

Melton
English, meaning 'town of Mel'.

Melva
Hawaiian, meaning 'plumeria'.

Melville
Scottish, meaning 'town of Mel'.

Melvin
(alt. Melvyn)
English, meaning 'smooth brow'.

Memphis
Greek, meaning 'established and beautiful'. Also the name of a city in the US.

Mercer
English, from the word 'mercer'.

Merl
French, meaning 'blackbird'.

Merlin
Welsh, meaning 'sea fortress'.

Merrick
Welsh, meaning 'Moorish'.

Merrill
Gaelic, meaning 'shining sea'.

Merritt
English, from the word 'merit'.

Merton
Old English, meaning 'town by the lake'.

Meyer
Hebrew, meaning 'bright farmer'.

Michael
Hebrew, meaning 'resembles God'. One of the archangels.

Michalis
Greek form of Michael, meaning 'resembles God'.

Michel
French form of Michael, meaning 'resembles God'.

Michelangelo
Italian, meaning 'Michael's angel'. Name of the famous painter.

Michele
Italian form of Michael, meaning 'resembles God'.

Michio
Japanese, meaning 'a man with the strength of three thousand men'.

Mickey
Variant of Michael meaning 'resembles God'. Often associated with the Disney character Mickey Mouse.

Miguel
Spanish form of Michael, meaning 'resembles God'.

Mike
Shortened form of Michael, meaning 'resembles God'.

Miklos
Greek form of Michael, meaning 'resembles God'.

Milan
From the name of the Italian city.

Miles
(alt. Milo, Milos, Myles)
English, from the word 'miles'.

Milton
English, meaning 'miller's town'. Also the name of the poet John Milton.

Miro
Slavic, meaning 'peace'.

Misha
Russian, meaning 'who is like God'.

Football players

Aaron (Lennon)
Alan (Shearer)
Ashley (Cole)
David (Beckham)
Frank (Lampard)
Gary (Lineker)
Jack (Wilshere)
Joe (Cole)
John (Terry)
Rio (Ferdinand)
Scott (Parker)
Steven (Gerrard)
Wayne (Rooney)

Mitch

Shortened form of Mitchell, meaning 'who is like God'.

Mitchell

English, meaning 'who is like God'.

Modesto

Italian, meaning 'modest'.

Moe

Hebrew, meaning 'God's helmet'.

Mohamed

(alt. Mohammad, Mohamet, Mohammed, Muhammad)
Arabic, meaning 'praiseworthy'.

Monroe

Gaelic, meaning 'mouth of the river Rotha'.

Monserrate

Latin, meaning 'jagged mountain'.

Montague

French, meaning 'pointed hill'.

Montana

Latin, meaning 'mountain'. Also a state in the US.

Monte

Italian, meaning 'mountain'.

Montgomery

Variant of Montague, meaning 'pointed hill'.

Monty

Shortened form of Montague, meaning 'pointed hill'.

M

Moody
English, from the word 'moody'.

Mordecai
Hebrew, meaning 'little man'.

Morgan
Welsh, meaning 'circling sea'.

Moritz
Latin, meaning 'dark skinned and Moorish'.

Moroccan
Arabic, meaning 'from Morocco'.

Morpheus
Greek, meaning 'shape'.

Morris
Welsh, meaning 'dark skinned and Moorish'.

Morrison
English, meaning 'son of Morris'.

Mortimer
French, meaning 'dead sea'.

Morton
Old English, meaning 'moor town'.

Moses
(alt. Moshe, Moshon)
Hebrew, meaning 'saviour'. In the Bible, Moses receives the Ten Commandments from God.

Moss
English, from the word 'moss'.

Muir
Gaelic, meaning 'of the moor'.

Mungo
Gaelic, meaning 'most dear'.

Murl
French, meaning 'blackbird'.

Murphy
Irish, meaning 'sea warrior'.

Murray
Gaelic, meaning 'lord and master'.

Mustafa
Arabic, meaning 'chosen'.

Mwita
African, meaning 'humourous one'.

Myron
Greek, meaning 'myrrh'.

Boys' names

Nairn
Scottish, meaning 'alder-tree river'.

Najee
Arabic, meaning 'dear companion'.

Nakia
Arabic, meaning 'pure'.

Nakul
Indian, meaning 'mongoose'.

Naphtali
Hebrew, meaning 'wrestling'.

Napoleon
Italian, meaning 'man from Naples'. Name of the French general who became Emperor of France.

Narciso
Latin, from the myth of Narcissus, famous for drowning after falling in love with his own reflection.

Nash
English, meaning 'at the ash tree'.

Nasir
Arabic, meaning 'helper'.

N

Popular song names

Adam ('Adam's Son', Blink 182)

Al ('You Can Call Me Al', Paul Simon)

Alejandro ('Alejandro', Lady Gaga)

Anthony ('Movin' Out', Billy Joel)

Daniel ('Daniel', Elton John)

Frankie ('Frankie', Sister Sledge)

Jimmy ('Jimmy Mack', Martha Reeves and the Vandellas)

Joe ('Hey Joe', Jimi Hendrix)

Maxwell ('Maxwell's Silver Hammer', The Beatles)

Robert ('Doctor Robert', The Beatles)

William ('William, It Was Really Nothing', The Smiths)

Nate
Hebrew, meaning 'God has given'.

Nathan
(alt. Nathaniel)
Hebrew, meaning 'God has given'.

Naval
Indian, meaning 'wonder'.

Naveen
Indian, meaning 'new'.

Neal
Irish, meaning 'champion'.

Ned
Nickname for Edward, meaning 'wealthy guard'.

Neftali
Hebrew, meaning 'struggling'.

Nehemiah
Hebrew, meaning 'comforter'.

Neil
(alt. Niall)
Irish, meaning 'champion'.

Neilson
Irish, meaning 'son of Neil'.

Nelson
Variant of Neil, meaning 'champion'.

N

Nemo
Latin, meaning 'nobody'.

Neo
Latin, meaning 'new'.

Nephi
Greek, meaning 'cloud'.

Nessim
Arabic, meaning 'breeze'.

Nestor
Greek, meaning 'traveller'.

Neville
Old French, meaning 'new village'.

Newland
(alt. Newlands, Newland, Neuland)
English, meaning 'from a new land'.

Newton
English, meaning 'new town'.

Nicholas
(alt. Niklas)
Greek, meaning 'victorious'.

Nick
(alt. Niko, Nikos, Nico)
Shortened form of Nicholas, meaning 'victorious'.

Nigel
Gaelic, meaning 'champion'.

Nikhil
Hindi, meaning 'whole' or 'entire'.

Nikita
Greek, meaning 'unconquered'. Also a girl's name.

Nikolai
Russian variant of Nicholas, meaning 'victorious'.

Nimrod
Hebrew, meaning 'we will rebel'.

Ninian
Gaelic, associated with the 5th-century saint of the same name.

Nissim
Hebrew, meaning 'wonderful things'.

Noah
Hebrew, meaning 'peaceful'.

Noel
French, meaning 'Christmas'.

Nolan
Gaelic, meaning 'champion'.

Norbert
Old German, meaning 'Northern brightness'.

Norman
Old German, meaning 'Northerner'.

Names of gods

Apollo (Music: Greek)
Eros (Love: Greek)
Hermes (Messenger of the gods: Greek)
Janus (Gates and Doors: Roman)
Mars (War: Roman)
Neptune (Sea: Roman)
Odin (Chief god: Norse)
Ra (Sun: Egyptian)
Thor (Thunder: Norse)

Normand
French, meaning 'from Normandy'.

Norris
Old French, meaning 'Northerner'.

Norton
English, meaning 'Northern town'.

Norval
French, meaning 'Northern town'.

Norwood
English, meaning 'Northern forest'.

Nova
Latin, meaning 'new'.

Nuno
Latin, meaning 'ninth'.

Nunzio
Italian, meaning 'messenger'.

Nyoka
African, meaning 'like a snake'.

 Boys' names

Oakley
English, meaning 'from the oak meadow'.

Obadiah
Hebrew, meaning 'God's worker'.

Obama
African, meaning 'crooked'. Made famous by the American President Barack Obama.

Obed
Hebrew, meaning 'servant of God'.

Popular French names

Alain	Jules
Alphonse	Louis
François	Noah
Gabriel	Nolan
Guy	Raphael
Jacques	Saber

Oberon

Old German, meaning 'royal bear'. The Fairy King in *A Midsummer Night's Dream*.

Obie

Shortened form of Oberon, meaning 'royal bear'.

Obijulu

African, meaning 'one who has been consoled'.

Octave

(alt. Octavian, Octavio)
Latin, meaning 'eight'.

Oda

(alt. Odell, Odie, Odis)
Hebrew, meaning 'praise God'.

Ogden

Old English, meaning 'oak valley'.

Oisin

(alt. Ossian)
Celtic, meaning 'fawn'. The name of an ancient Irish poet.

Ola

Norse, meaning 'precious'.

Olaf

(alt. Olan)
Old Norse, meaning 'ancestor'.

Oleander

Hawaiian, meaning 'joyous'.

Oleg

(alt. Olen)
Russian, meaning 'holy'.

Olin

Russian, meaning 'rock'.

Oliver

Latin, meaning 'olive tree'. The UK's most popular boy's name in 2011.

Olivier

French form of Oliver, meaning 'olive tree'.

Ollie

Shortened form of Oliver, meaning 'olive tree'.

Omar

(alt. Omari, Omarion)
Arabic, meaning 'speaker'.

Ondrej

Czech, meaning 'manly'.

O

Ora
Latin, meaning 'hour'.

Oran
(alt. Oren, Orrin)
Gaelic, meaning 'light and pale'.

Orange
English, from the word 'orange'.

Orion
From the Greek hunter.

Orlando
(alt. Orlo)
Old German, meaning 'old land'. Name of a city in the US.

Orpheus
Greek, meaning 'beautiful voice'.

Orrick
English, meaning 'sword ruler'.

Orson
Latin, meaning 'bear'.

Orville
Old French, meaning 'gold town'.

Osaka
From the Japanese city.

Osborne
Norse, meaning 'bear god'.

Oscar
Old English, meaning 'spear of the Gods'.

Osias
Hebrew, meaning 'salvation'.

Foreign alternatives
David – Dafydd, Davin
Francis – Francisco, Paco
John – Jean, Giovanni, Juan
Michael – Miguel, Mikhail
Peter – Pedro, Pierre, Pyotr, Piers
Rory – Ruaridh

O

Oswald
German, meaning 'God's power'.

Otha
(alt. Otho)
German, meaning 'wealth'.

Othello
Old German, meaning 'wealth'. From the Shakespearean character.

Otis
German, meaning 'wealth'.

Otten
English, meaning 'otter-like'.

Otto
Italian, meaning 'eight'.

Ovid
Latin, meaning 'sheep'. Associated with the Roman poet.

Owain
Welsh, meaning 'youth'.

Owen
Welsh, meaning 'well born and noble'.

Oz
Hebrew, meaning 'strength'.

Palindrome names

Bob
Ebbe
Kuruk
Masam
Neven
Okko
Otto
Pip
Ramar
Uku

Boys' names

Pablo
Spanish, meaning 'little'.

Paco
Native American, meaning 'eagle'. Also a Spanish alternative for Francisco.

Padma
Sanskrit, meaning 'lotus'.

Padraig
Irish, meaning 'noble'.

Panos
Greek, meaning 'all holy'.

Paolo
Italian, meaning 'little'.

Paresh
Indian, meaning 'supreme standard'.

Paris
From France's capital city. Also the Trojan prince in Homer's *Iliad* and Juliet's suitor in Shakespeare's *Romeo and Juliet*.

Pascal
Latin, meaning 'Easter child'.

Pat
Shortened form of Patrick, meaning 'noble'.

Patrice
Variant of Patrick, meaning 'noble'.

P

Patrick
Irish, meaning 'noble'.

Patten
English, meaning 'noble'.

Paul
Hebrew, meaning 'small'.

Pavel
Latin, meaning 'small'.

Pax
Latin, meaning 'peace'.

Paxton
English, meaning 'town of peace'.

Payne
Latin, meaning 'peasant'.

Payton
Latin, meaning 'peasant's town'.

Pedro
Spanish form of Peter, meaning 'rock'.

Penn
English, meaning 'hill'.

Percival
French, meaning 'pierce the valley'.

Percy
Shortened form of Percival, meaning 'pierce the valley'.

Perez
Hebrew, meaning 'breach'.

Pericles
Greek, meaning 'far-famed'.

Perrin
Greek, meaning 'rock'.

Perry
English, meaning 'rock'.

Pervis
English, meaning 'purveyor'.

Pesah
(alt. Pesach, Pesasch)
Hebrew, meaning 'spared'.

Pete
Shortened form of Peter, meaning 'rock'.

P

Peter

Greek, meaning 'rock'.

Petros

Greek form of Peter, meaning 'rock'.

Peyton

Old English, meaning 'fighting man's estate'.

Phil

Shortened form of Philip, meaning 'lover of horses'.

Philemon

Greek, meaning 'affectionate'.

Philip

(alt. Phillip)

Greek, meaning 'lover of horses'.

Philo

Greek, meaning 'love'.

Phineas

(alt. Pinchas)

Hebrew, meaning 'oracle'.

Phoenix

Greek, meaning 'dark red'.

Pierre

French form of Peter, meaning 'rock'.

Piers

Greek form of Peter, meaning 'rock'.

Pierson

Variant of Pierce, meaning 'son of Piers'.

Pip

Greek, shortened form of Philip, meaning 'lover of horses'.

No-nickname names

Alex
Beau
Cole
Hugh
Jude
Keith
Miles
Morgan
Otto
Owen
Toby

P

Placido
Latin, meaning 'placid'.

Pradeep
Hindi, meaning 'light'.

Pranav
Hindi, meaning 'spiritual leader'.

Presley
Old English, meaning 'priest's meadow'.

Preston
Old English, meaning 'priest's town'.

Primo
Italian, meaning 'first'.

Primus
Latin, meaning 'first'.

Prince
English, from the word 'prince'.

Proctor
(alt. Prockter, Procter)
Latin, meaning 'steward'.

Popular South American names

Accius
Alban
Arrian
Coatl
Lucas
Matlal
Rafael
Tuco
Vincent
Zolin

Prospero
Latin, meaning 'prosperous'.

Pryor
English, meaning 'first'.

Ptolemy
Greek, meaning 'aggressive' or 'warlike'.

Purvis
(alt. Purves, Purviss)
French, meaning 'purveyor'.

 Boys' names

Qino
Chinese, meaning 'handsome'.

Quabil
Arabic, meaning 'able'.

Quadim
Arabic, meaning 'able'.

Quadir
Arabic, meaning 'powerful'.

Quaid
Irish, meaning 'fourth'.

Qued
Native American, meaning 'weaver of a decorated robe'.

Quemby
Norse, meaning 'from the woman's estate'.

Quentin
(alt. Quinten, Quintin, Quinton, Quintus)
Latin, meaning 'fifth'.

Quillan
Gaelic, meaning 'sword'.

Quillon
Gaelic, meaning 'club'.

Quincy
Old French, meaning 'estate of the fifth son'.

Quinlan

Gaelic, meaning 'fit, shapely and strong'.

Quinn

Gaelic, meaning 'counsel'.

Quinton

English, meaning 'queen's community'.

Popular North American names

Alexander
Anthony
Daniel
Ethan
Jacob
Jayden
Joshua
Michael
Noah
William

 Boys' names

Radames

Slavic, meaning 'famous joy'.

Raekwon

Hebrew, meaning 'God has healed'.

Rafael

(alt. Rafe, Rafer, Raffi, Raphael)

Hebrew, meaning 'God has healed'. One of the archangels.

Ragnar

Old Norse, meaning 'judgement warrior'.

Raheem

Arabic, meaning 'merciful and kind'.

Rahm

Hebrew, meaning 'pleasing'.

Rahul

(alt. Raoul, Raul)

Indian, meaning 'efficient'.

Raiden

(alt. Rainen)

From the Japanese god of thunder.

Rainer

Old German, meaning 'deciding warrior'.

Raj

Indian, meaning 'king'.

Rajesh

(alt. Ramesh)

Indian, meaning 'ruler of kings'.

R

Raleigh

Old English, meaning 'deer's meadow'.

Ralph

Old English, meaning 'wolf'.

Ram

English, from the word 'ram'.

Ramiro

Germanic, meaning 'powerful in battle'.

Ramone

Spanish, meaning 'wise supporter' or 'romantic'.

Ramsey

(alt. Ramsay)

Old English, meaning 'wild garlic island'.

Randall

(alt. Randolph)

Old German, meaning 'wolf shield'.

Randy

Variant of Randall, meaning 'wolf shield'. In modern English, randy can also mean amorous.

Raniel

English, meaning 'God is my happiness'.

Ranjit

Indian, meaning 'influenced by charm'.

Rannoch

Gaelic, meaning 'fern'.

Rashad

Arabic, meaning 'good judgment'.

Rasheed

(alt. Rashid)

Indian, meaning 'rightly guided'.

Rasmus

Greek, meaning 'beloved'.

Raven

English, from the word 'raven'.

Ravi

French, meaning 'delighted'.

Rawlins

French alternative of Roland, meaning 'renowned land'.

R

Ray

English, from the word 'ray'.

Raymond
(alt. Rayner)

English, meaning 'advisor'.

Raz

Israeli, meaning 'secret' or 'mystery'.

Reagan

Irish, meaning 'little king'.

Reggie

Latin, meaning 'regal'.

Reginald

Latin, meaning 'regal'.

Regis

Shortened form of Reginald, meaning 'regal'.

Reid

Old English, meaning 'by the reeds'.

Reilly
(alt. Riley)

English, meaning 'courageous'.

Remington

English, meaning 'ridge town'.

Remus

Latin, meaning 'swift'.

Rémy

French, meaning 'from Rheims'.

Ren

Shortened form of Reginald, meaning 'regal'.

Renato

Latin, meaning 'rebirth'.

Rene

French, meaning 'rebirth'.

Popular Irish names

Brian
Cian
Connor
Eoin
Finn
Kieran
Niall
Patrick
Ronan
Sean

Reno

Latin, meaning 'renewed'.

Reuben

Spanish, meaning 'a son'.

Reuel

Hebrew, meaning 'friend of God'.

Rex

Latin, meaning 'king'.

Rey

Spanish, meaning 'king'.

Reynold

Latin, meaning 'king's advisor'.

Rhodes

German, meaning 'where the roses grow'. Also the name of the Greek town.

Rhodri

Welsh, meaning 'ruler of the circle'.

Rhys
(alt. Reece)

Welsh, meaning 'enthusiasm'.

Ricardo

Spanish form of Richard, meaning 'powerful leader'.

Richard

Old German, meaning 'powerful leader'.

Richie

Shortened form of Richard, meaning 'powerful leader'.

Rick
(alt. Ricki, Ricky)

Shortened form of Richard, meaning 'powerful leader'.

Ridley

English, meaning 'cleared wood'.

Rigby

English, meaning 'valley of the ruler'.

Ringo

English, meaning 'ring'.

Rio

Spanish, meaning 'river'.

Riordan

Gaelic, meaning 'bard'.

Rishi

Variant of Richard, meaning 'powerful leader'.

Ritchie

Shortened form of Richard, meaning 'powerful leader'.

River

Latin, meaning 'river'.

Roald

Scandinavian, meaning 'ruler'.

Rob

Shortened form of Robert, meaning 'bright fame'.

Robbie

Shortened form of Robert, meaning 'bright fame'.

Robert

Old German, meaning 'bright fame'.

Roberto

Italian form of Robert, meaning 'bright fame'.

Robin

English, from the word 'robin'.

Robinson

English, meaning 'son of Robin'.

Rocco

(alt. Rocky)

Italian, meaning 'rest'.

Rockwell

English, meaning 'of the rock well'.

Rod

Short for Rhodri, Roderick and Rodney.

Roderick

German, meaning 'famous power'.

Rodney

Old German, meaning 'island near the clearing'.

Rodrigo

Spanish form of Roderick, meaning 'famous power'.

R

Roger

Old German, meaning 'spear man'.

Roland

Old German, meaning 'renowned land'.

Rolf

Old German, meaning 'wolf'.

Rollie
(alt. Rollo)

Old German, meaning 'renowned land'.

Roman

Latin, meaning 'from Rome'.

Romeo

Latin, meaning 'pilgrim to Rome'. Made famous by Shakespeare's play.

Ron
(alt. Ronnie)

Shortened form of Ronald, meaning 'mountain of strength'.

Ronald

Norse, meaning 'mountain of strength'.

Ronan

Gaelic, meaning 'little seal'.

Rory

English, meaning 'red king'.

Ross
(alt. Russ)

Scottish, meaning 'cape'.

Rowan
(alt. Roan)

Gaelic, meaning 'little red one'. Also reference to the rowan tree.

Roy

Gaelic, meaning 'red'.

Popular Scottish names

Alastair
Angus
Callum
Cameron
Douglas
Fraser
Hamish
Malcolm
Roderick
Stuart

R

Ruben

Hebrew, meaning 'son'.

Rudolph

Old German, meaning 'famous wolf'.

Rudy

Shortened form of Rudolph, meaning 'famous wolf'.

Rufus

Latin, meaning 'red-haired'.

Rupert

Variant of Robert, meaning 'bright fame'.

Ruslan

Russian, meaning 'like a lion'.

Russell

Old French, meaning 'little red one'.

Rusty

English, meaning 'ruddy'.

Ryan

Gaelic, meaning 'little king'.

Ryder

English, meaning 'horseman'.

Rye

English, from the word 'rye'.

Ryker

From Richard, meaning 'powerful leader'.

Rylan

English, meaning 'land where rye is grown'.

Ryley

Old English, meaning 'rye clearing'.

Ryu

Japanese, meaning 'dragon'.

 Boys' names

S

Saar
Hebrew, meaning 'tempest'.

Saber
French, meaning 'sword'.

Sagar
African, meaning 'ruler of the water'.

Sage
English, meaning 'wise'.

Sakari
Native American, meaning 'sweet'.

Salil
Indian, meaning 'from the water'.

Salim
Arabic, meaning 'secure'.

Salvador
Spanish, meaning 'saviour'.

Salvatore
Italian, meaning 'saviour'.

Nautical names

Caspian
Dylan
Merlin
Murphy
Neptune

Sam
(alt. Sama, Sammie, Sammy)
Hebrew, meaning 'God is heard'. Shortened form of Samuel.

Samir
Arabic, meaning 'pleasant companion'.

Samson
Hebrew, meaning 'son of Sam'.

Samuel
Hebrew, meaning 'God is heard'.

Sandeep
Indian, meaning 'lighting the way'.

Sandro
Shortened form of Alessandro, meaning 'defending men'.

Sandy
Shortened form of Alexander, meaning 'defending men'.

Sanjay
Indian, meaning 'victory'.

Santiago
Spanish, meaning 'Saint James'.

Santino
Spanish, meaning 'little Saint James'.

Santo
(alt. Santos)
Latin, meaning 'saint'.

Sasha
(alt. Sacha)
Shortened Russian form of Alexander, meaning 'defending men'.

Scott
(alt. Scottie)
English, meaning 'from Scotland'.

Seamus
Irish variant of James, meaning 'he who supplants'.

Sean
(alt. Shaun)
Variant of John, meaning 'God is gracious'.

Sebastian
Greek, meaning 'revered'.

S

Sébastien
French form of Sebastian, meaning 'revered'.

Sergio
Latin, meaning 'servant'.

Seth
Hebrew, meaning 'appointed'.

Severus
Latin, meaning 'severe'. Made popular by the character Severus Snape in the Harry Potter series.

Seymour
English, from Saint-Maur in northern France.

Shalen
Arabic, meaning 'tribal leader'.

Shane
Variant of Sean, meaning 'God is gracious'.

Sharif
Arabic, meaning 'honoured'.

Shea
Gaelic, meaning 'admirable'.

Shelby
Norse, meaning 'willow'.

Sherlock
English, meaning 'fair haired'.

Sherman
Old English, meaning 'shear man'.

Shmuel
Hebrew, meaning 'his name is God'.

Shola
Arabic, meaning 'energetic'.

Sid
Shortened form of Sidney, meaning 'wide meadow'.

Names of painters

Claude (Monet)
Francis (Bacon)
Leonardo (da Vinci)
Paul (Cezanne)
Salvador (Dali)
Vincent (Van Gogh)

S

Sidney
English, meaning 'wide meadow'.

Sigmund
Old German, meaning 'victorious hand'.

Silvanus
(alt. Silvio)
Latin, meaning 'woods'.

Sim
Swahili, shortened form of Simba, meaning 'lion'.

Simba
Swahili, meaning 'lion'.

Simon
(alt. Simeon)
Hebrew, meaning 'to hear'.

Sinbad
Persian, meaning 'Lord of Sages'. Literary merchant adventurer.

Sindri
Norse, meaning 'dwarf'.

Sipho
African, meaning 'the unknown one'.

Sire
English, from the word 'sire'.

Sirius
Hebrew, meaning 'brightest star'. Name of Harry Potter's godfather, Sirius Black.

Skipper
English, meaning 'ship captain'.

Skyler
English, meaning 'scholar'.

Solomon
Hebrew, meaning 'peace'.

Popular Australian names

Cooper
Ethan
Jack
Joshua
Lachlan
Noah
Oliver
Riley
Thomas
William

S

Sonny
American English, meaning 'son'.

Soren
Scandinavian, meaning 'brightest star'.

Spencer
English, meaning 'dispenser'.

Spike
English, from the word 'spike'.

Stamos
Greek, meaning 'reasonable'.

Stan
Shortened form of Stanley, meaning 'stony meadow'.

Stanford
English, meaning 'stone ford'.

Stanley
English, meaning 'stony meadow'.

Stavros
Greek, meaning 'crowned'.

Stellan
Latin, meaning 'starred'.

Steno
German, meaning 'stone'.

Stephen
(alt. *Stefan, Stefano, Steffan*)
English, meaning 'crowned'.

Steven
(alt. *Steve, Stevie*)
English, meaning 'crowned'.

Stewart
English, meaning 'steward'.

Stoney
English, meaning 'stone like'.

Storm
English, from the word 'storm'.

Peaceful names

Glade
Manfred
Paxton
Vale
Wilfred

S

Stuart
English, meaning 'steward'.

Sven
Norse, meaning 'boy'.

Sydney
English, meaning 'wide meadow'. Also a city in Australia.

Syed
Arabic, meaning 'lucky'.

Sylvester
Latin, meaning 'wooded'.

Syon
Indian, meaning 'followed by good'.

T Boys' names

Tacitus

Latin, meaning 'silent, calm'. From the Roman historian.

Tad

English, from the word 'tadpole'.

Taine

Gaelic, meaning 'river'.

Taj

Indian, meaning 'crown'.

Takashi

Japanese, meaning 'praiseworthy'.

Takoda

Sioux, meaning 'friend to everyone'.

Talbot

(alt. Tal)

English, meaning 'command of the valley'. An aristocratic name.

Tamir

Arabic, meaning 'tall and wealthy'.

Taras

(alt. Tarez)

Scottish, meaning 'crag'.

Tarek

Arabic, meaning 'evening caller'.

Tarian

Welsh, meaning 'silver'.

Tariq

Arabic, meaning 'morning star'.

T

Tarquin
Latin, from the Roman clan name.

Tarun
Hindi, meaning 'young'.

Tatanka
Hebrew, meaning 'bull'.

Tate
English, meaning 'cheerful'.

Taurean
English, meaning 'bull like'.

Tavares
English, meaning 'descendant of the hermit'.

Tave
(alt. Tavian, Tavis, Tavish)
French, from Gustave, meaning 'royal staff'.

Tavor
Hebrew, meaning 'misfortunate'.

Taylor
English, meaning 'tailor'.

Ted
(alt. Teddy)
English, from Edward, meaning 'wealthy guard'.

Tennessee
Native American, meaning 'river town'.

Terence
(alt. Terrill, Terry)
English, meaning 'tender'.

Tex
English, meaning 'Texan'.

Thabo
African, meaning 'filled with happiness'.

Thane
(alt. Thayer)
Scottish, meaning 'landholder'.

Popular Asian names

Chang
Fang
Hiro
Hiroshi
Kane
Koji
Rei
Shin
Yemon
Zinan

Thelonius
Latin, meaning 'ruler of the people'.

Theo
Shortened form of Theodore, meaning 'God's gift'.

Theodore
Greek, meaning 'God's gift'.

Theophile
Latin, meaning 'God's love'.

Theron
Greek, meaning 'hunter'.

Thierry
French variant of Terence, meaning 'tender'.

Thomas
Aramaic, meaning 'twin'.

Thomsen
English, meaning 'son of Thomas'.

Thor
Norse, meaning 'thunder'.

Tiago
From Santiago, meaning 'Saint James'.

Tibor
Latin, from the river Tiber.

Tieman
Gaelic, meaning 'lord'.

Tien
Vietnamese, meaning 'first'.

Tim
Shortened form of Timothy, meaning 'God's honour'.

Timothy
Greek, meaning 'God's honour'.

Tito
(alt. Titus)
Latin, meaning 'defender'.

Tobias
(alt. Toby)
Hebrew, meaning 'God is good'.

Tod
(alt. Todd)
English, meaning 'fox'.

Tom
(alt. Tomlin, Tommy)
Aramaic, meaning 'twin'.

T

Tonneau
French, meaning 'barrel'.

Tony
Shortened form of Anthony, from the old Roman family name.

Torey
Norse, meaning 'Thor'.

Torin
Gaelic, meaning 'chief'.

Torquil
Gaelic, meaning 'helmet'.

Toshi
Japanese, meaning 'reflection'.

Travis
French, meaning 'crossover'.

Trevelian
Welsh, meaning 'of the house of Eden'.

Trevor
Welsh, meaning 'great settlement'.

Trey
(alt. Tyree)
French, meaning 'very'.

Tristan
(alt. Tristram)
Celtic, from the Celtic hero.

Troy
Gaelic, meaning 'descended from the soldier'.

Tudor
Variant of Theodore, 'God's gift'.

Tyler
English, meaning 'tile maker'.

Tyrell
French, meaning 'puller'.

Tyrone
Gaelic, meaning 'Owen's county'.

Tyson
English, meaning 'son of Tyrone'.

Famous rugby players

Brian (O'Driscoll)
Gavin (Henson)
Jonny (Wilkinson)
Lawrence (Dallaglio)
Martin (Johnson)
Thom (Evans)
Toby (Flood)

 Boys' names

Uberto
(alt. Umberto)
Italian, variant of Hubert, meaning 'bright or shining intellect'.

Udath
(alt. Udathel)
Indian, meaning 'noble'.

Udo
German, meaning 'power of the wolf'.

Ugo
Italian form of Hugo, meaning 'mind and heart'.

Ulf
German, meaning 'wolf'.

Ulrich
German, meaning 'noble ruler'.

Ultan
Irish, meaning 'from Ulster'.

Ulysses
Greek, meaning 'wrathful'. Made famous by the mythological voyager.

Unwyn
(alt. Unwin, Unwine)
English, meaning 'unfriendly'.

Upton
English, meaning 'high town'.

Urho
Finnish, meaning 'brave'.

Uri

(alt. Uriah, Urias)

Hebrew, meaning 'my light'.

Uriel

Hebrew, meaning 'angel of light'. One of the archangels.

Usher

English, from the word 'usher'. Made famous by the American R&B star.

Uttam

Indian, meaning 'best'.

Uzi

Hebrew, meaning 'my strength'.

Uzzi

(alt. Uzziah)

Hebrew, meaning 'my power'.

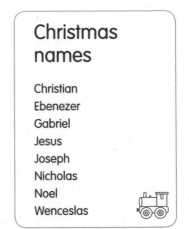

Christmas names

Christian
Ebenezer
Gabriel
Jesus
Joseph
Nicholas
Noel
Wenceslas

Boys' names

Vaclav
Czech, meaning 'receives glory'.

Vadim
Russian, meaning 'scandal maker'.

Valdemar
German, meaning 'renowned leader'.

Valente
Latin, meaning 'valiant'.

Valentin
(alt. Val)
French, meaning 'valentine'.

Valentine
English, from the word 'valentine'.

Valentino
Italian, meaning 'valentine'.

Valerio
Italian, meaning 'valiant'.

Valia
Indian, meaning 'king of the monkeys'.

Van
Dutch, meaning 'son of'.

Vance
English, meaning 'marshland'.

V

Vangelis
Greek, meaning 'good news'.

Varro
Latin, meaning 'strong'.

Varun
Hindi, meaning 'water god'.

Vasilis
Greek, meaning 'kingly'.

Vaughan
Welsh, meaning 'little'.

Vernell
French, meaning 'green and flourishing'.

Verner
German, meaning 'army defender'.

Vernon
(alt. Vernie)
French, meaning 'alder grove'.

Versilius
Latin, meaning 'flier'.

Vester
Latin, meaning 'wooded'.

Vibol
Cambodian, meaning 'man of plenty'.

Shakespearean names

Angelo *(Measure for Measure)*
Anthony *(Anthony and Cleopatra)*
Balthazar *(Romeo and Juliet)*
Hamlet *(Hamlet)*
Henry *(Henry V)*
Iago *(Othello)*
Othello *(Othello)*
Richard *(Richard III)*
Romeo *(Romeo and Juliet)*
Sebastian *(Twelfth Night)*

Victor
Latin, meaning 'champion'.

Vidal
(alt. Vidar)
Spanish, meaning 'life giving'.

Vijay
Hindi, meaning 'conquering'.

Vikram
Hindi, meaning 'sun'.

Viktor
Latin, meaning 'victory'.

Ville
French, meaning 'town'.

Vincent
(alt. Vince)
English, meaning 'victorious'.

Virgil
Latin, meaning 'staff bearer'.
From the Latin poet.

Vito
Spanish, meaning 'life'.

Vittorio
Italian, meaning 'victory'.

Vitus
Latin, meaning 'life'.

Vivek
Indian, meaning 'wisdom'.

Vivian
Latin, meaning 'lively'.

Vladimir
Slavic, meaning 'prince'.

Volker
German, meaning 'defender of
the people'.

Von
Norse, meaning 'hope'.

W

Boys' names

Wade
English, meaning 'to move forward' or 'to go'.

Waldemar
German, meaning 'famous ruler'.

Walden
English, meaning 'valley of the Britons'.

Waldo
Old German, meaning 'rule'.

Walker
English, meaning 'a fuller'.

Wallace
English, meaning 'foreigner' or 'stranger'.

Wally
German, meaning 'ruler of the army'.

Walter
(alt. Walt)
German, meaning 'ruler of the army'.

Wasim
Arabic, meaning 'attractive' or 'full of grace'.

Ward
English, meaning 'guardian'.

Wardell
Old English, meaning 'watchman's hill'.

Warner

German, meaning 'army guard'.

Warren

German, meaning 'guard' or 'the game park'.

Warwick

English, meaning 'farm near the weir'.

Washington

English, meaning 'clever' or 'clever man's settlement'.

Wassily

Greek, meaning 'royal' or 'kingly'.

Watson

English, meaning 'son' or 'son of Walter'.

Waverley
(alt. Waverly)

English, meaning 'quaking aspen'.

Waylon

English, meaning 'land by the road'.

Wayne

English, meaning 'a cartwright'.

Webster

English, meaning 'weaver'.

Weldon

English, meaning 'from the hill of well' or 'hill with a well'.

Wendell
(alt. Wendel)

German, meaning 'a wend'.

Werner

German, meaning 'army guard'.

Werther

German, meaning 'a soldier in the army'.

Weston

English, meaning 'from the west town'.

Wheeler

English, meaning 'wheel maker'.

Whitley

English, meaning 'white wood'.

Whitman

Old English, meaning 'white man'.

Whitney

Old English, meaning 'white island'.

Wilber
(alt. Wilbur)

Old German, meaning 'bright will'.

Wildon

English, meaning 'wooded hill'.

Wiley

Old English, meaning 'beguiling' or 'enchanting'.

Wilford

Old English, meaning 'the ford by the willows'.

Wilfredo
(alt. Wilfred, Wilfrid)

English, meaning 'to will peace'.

Wilhelm

German, meaning 'strong-willed warrior'.

Wilkes
(alt. Wilkie)

Old English, meaning 'strong-willed protector' or 'strong and resolute protector'.

William
(alt. Will, Willie, Willy)

English (Teutonic), meaning 'strong protector' or 'strong-willed warrior'.

Willis

English, meaning 'server of William'.

Willoughby

Old Norse and Old English, meaning 'from the farm by the trees'.

Wilmer

English (Teutonic), meaning 'famously resolute'.

Wilmot

English, meaning 'resolute mind'.

Wilson

English, meaning 'son of William'.

Wilton

Old Norse and English, meaning 'from the farm by the brook' or 'from the farm by the streams'.

Windell

(alt. Wendell)

German, meaning 'wanderer' or 'seeker'.

Windsor

Old English, meaning 'river bank' or 'landing place'.

Winfield

English, meaning 'from the field of Wina'.

Winslow

Old English, meaning 'victory on the hill'.

Winter

Old English, meaning 'to be born in the winter'.

Winthrop

Old English, meaning 'village of friends'.

Knights of the round table

Arthur
Gareth
Gawain
Lancelot
Tristram

Winton

Old English, meaning 'a friend's farm'.

Wirrin

Aboriginal, meaning 'a tea tree'.

Wistan

Old English, meaning 'battle stone' or 'mark of the battle'.

Wittan

Old English, meaning 'farm in the woods' or 'farm by the woods'.

Wolf

(alt. Wolfe)

English, meaning 'strong as a wolf'.

W

Wolfgang

Teutonic, meaning 'the path of wolves'.

Wolfrom

Teutonic, meaning 'raven wolf'.

Wolter

Dutch, a form of Walter meaning 'ruler of the army'.

Woodburn

Old English, meaning 'a stream in the woods'.

Woodrow

English, meaning 'from the row of houses by the wood'.

Woodward

English, meaning 'guardian of the forest'.

Woody

American, meaning 'path in the woods'.

Worcester

Old English, meaning 'from a Roman site'.

Worth

American, meaning 'worth much' or 'wealthy place' or 'wealth and riches'.

Wren

Old English, meaning 'tiny bird'.

Wright

Old English, meaning 'to be a craftsman' or 'from a carpenter'.

Wyatt

Teutonic, meaning 'from wood' or 'from the wide water'.

Wyclef

(alt. Wycleff, Wycliff, Wycliffe)

English, meaning 'inhabitant of the white cliff'.

Wynn

(alt. Wyn)

Welsh, meaning 'very blessed' or 'the fair blessed one'.

Popular Welsh names

Aeron	Evan
Aled	Gareth
Bryn	Gwyn
Dafydd	Owain
Dai	Rhys
Dylan	Wallace

 Boys' names

 X

Xadrian

American, a combination of X and Adrian, meaning 'from Hadria'.

Xander

Greek, meaning 'defender of the people'.

Xannon

American, meaning 'descendant of an ancient family'.

Xanthus

Greek, meaning 'golden-haired'.

Xavier

Latin, meaning 'to the new house'.

Xenon

Greek, meaning 'the guest'.

Xerxes

Persian, meaning 'ruler of the people' or 'respected king'.

Xeven

Slavic, meaning 'lively'.

Xylander

Greek, meaning 'man of the forest'.

Bird names

Gannet
Phoenix
Robin
Tern
Wren

Boys' names

Yaal

Hebrew, meaning 'ascending' or 'one to ascend'.

Yadid

Hebrew, meaning 'the beloved one'.

Yadon

Hebrew, meaning 'against judgment'.

Yahir

Spanish, meaning 'handsome one'.

Yaholo

Native American, meaning 'yells'.

Yair

Hebrew, meaning 'the enlightening one' or 'illuminating'.

Yakiya

Hebrew, meaning 'pure' or 'bright'.

Yanis

(alt. Yannis)

Greek, a form of John meaning 'gift of God'.

Yarden

Hebrew, meaning 'to flow downward'.

Ye

Chinese, meaning 'bright one' or 'light'.

Yehuda

Hebrew, meaning 'to praise and exalt'.

Yered

Hebrew, a form of Jared, meaning 'descending'.

Yerik

Russian, meaning 'God-appointed one'.

Yerodin

African, meaning 'studious'.

Yervant

Armenian, meaning 'king of people'.

Yitzak
(alt. Yitzaak)

Hebrew, meaning 'laughter' or 'one who laughs'.

Ynyr

Welsh, meaning 'to honour'.

Yobachi

African, meaning 'one who prays to God' or 'prayed to God'.

Yogi

Japanese, meaning 'one who practises yoga' or 'from yoga'.

Yoloti

Aztec, meaning 'heart'.

Yona

Native American, meaning 'bear'; and also Hebrew, meaning 'dove'.

York

Celtic, meaning 'yew tree' or 'from the farm of the yew tree'.

Yosef

Hebrew, meaning 'added by God' or 'God shall add'.

Yuri

Aboriginal, meaning 'to hear'; Japanese, meaning 'one to listen'; Russian, a form of George meaning 'farmer'.

Yuuta

Japanese, meaning 'excellent'.

Yves

French, meaning 'miniature archer' or 'small archer'.

Z

Boys' names

Zachariah
(alt. Zac, Zach, Zachary)
Hebrew, meaning 'remembered by the Lord' or 'God has remembered'.

Zad
Persian, meaning 'my son'.

Zada
(alt. Zadan, Zadin, Zadun)
Dutch, meaning 'a man who sowed seeds'.

Zadok
Hebrew, meaning 'righteous one'.

Zador
Hungarian, meaning 'violent demeanour'.

Zafar
Arabic, meaning 'triumphant'.

Zaid
African, meaning 'increase the growth' or 'growth'.

Popular Spanish names

Alejandro
Carlos
Diego
Ivan
Javier
Jorge
Marcos
Mario
Pablo
Raul

Z

Zaide

Yiddish, meaning 'the elder ones'.

Zain

(alt. Zane)

Arabic, meaning 'the handsome son'.

Zaire

African, meaning 'river from Zaire'.

Zander

Greek, meaning 'defender of my people'.

Zarek

Persian, meaning 'God protect our King'.

Zoltan

(alt. Zoltin)

Hungarian, meaning 'life'.

Zuma

Arabic, meaning 'peace'.

Fiery names

Aidan
Blaze
Flint
Kegan
Kenneth

part three

Girls' Names

A Girls' names

A'mari

Variation of the Swahili or Muslim name Amira, meaning 'princess'.

Aanya

Variation of the Russian name Anya, meaning 'favour' or 'grace'. Also Sanskrit, meaning 'the inexhaustible'.

Aaryanna

Derivative of the Latin and Greek name Ariadne, both meaning 'the very holy one'.

Abby

(alt. Abbey, Abbie)

Hebrew Form of Abigail, meaning 'my father's joy'.

Abigail

(alt. Abagail, Abbiegayle, Abbigail, Abigale, Abigayle)

Hebrew, meaning 'my father's joy'.

Abilene

(alt. Abilee)

Latin and Spanish for 'hazelnut'.

Abina

(alt. Abena)

Ghanaian, meaning 'born on Tuesday'.

Abra

Female variation of Abraham. Also Sanskrit, meaning 'clouds'.

Abril

Spanish for the month of April. Also Latin, meaning 'open'.

Acacia

Greek, meaning 'point' or 'thorn'. Also a species of flowering trees and shrubs.

Acadia

Variation of the Greek word arcadia meaning 'paradise'. Originally, a French colony in Canada.

Ada

(alt. Adair)

Hebrew, meaning 'adornment'.

Adalee

German, meaning 'noble'.

Adalia

Hebrew, meaning 'God is my refuge'.

Addie

(alt. Addy, Adi)

Shortened form of Addison, Adelaide, Adele and Adeline.

Addison

(alt. Addisyn, Addyson)

English, meaning 'son of Adam'.

Adelaide

(alt. Adelaida)

German, popular after the rule of William IV and Queen Adelaide of England in the 19th century.

Adele

(alt. Adela, Adelia, Adell, Adella, Adelle)

German, meaning 'noble' or 'nobility'.

Adeline

(alt. Adalyn, Adalynn, Adelina, Adelyn)

Variant of Adelaide, meaning 'noble'.

Aden

(alt. Addien)

Hebrew, meaning 'decoration'.

Adeola

(alt. Adeolah, Adeolla)

African, meaning 'weaver of a crown of honour'.

Aderyn

Welsh, meaning 'bird'.

Adesina

Nigerian, meaning 'she paves the way'. Usually given to a firstborn daughter.

Adia

Variant of Ada, meaning 'adornment'.

Adina
(alt. Adena)

Hebrew, meaning 'high hopes' or 'precious'.

Adira

Hebrew, meaning 'noble' or 'powerful'.

Adrian

Italian, from the northern city of Hadria.

Adrianna
(alt. Adriana)

Variant of Adrienne, meaning 'rich' or 'dark'.

Adrienne
(alt. Adriane, Adrianne)

Greek, meaning 'rich', or Latin, meaning 'dark'.

Aegle

Greek, meaning 'brightness' or 'splendour'.

Movie inspirations

Bella (*Twilight*)
Cady (*Mean Girls*)
Fiona (*Shrek*)
Holly (*Breakfast at Tiffany's*)
Katniss (*The Hunger Games*)
Lara (*Tomb Raider*)
Maria (*The Sound of Music*)
Marla (*Fight Club*)
Mary (*Mary Poppins*)
Nina (*Black Swan*)
Pandora (*Avatar*)
Trinity (*The Matrix*)

Aerin
Variant of Erin, meaning 'peace-making'.

Aerith
American, from a character in the computer game *Final Fantasy VII*.

Aero
(alt. Aeron)
Greek, meaning 'water'.

Aerolynn
Combination of the Greek Aero, meaning 'water', and the English Lynn, meaning 'waterfall'.

Afia
(alt. Aff, Affi)
Arabic, meaning 'a child born on Friday'.

Africa
Celtic, meaning 'pleasant', as well as the name of the continent.

Afsaneh
Iranian, meaning 'a fairy tale'.

Afsha
Persian, meaning 'one who sprinkles light'.

Afton
Originally a place name in Scotland.

Agatha
From Saint Agatha, the patron saint of bells, meaning 'good'.

Aglaia
One of the three Greek Graces, meaning 'brilliance'.

Agnes
Greek, meaning 'virginal' or 'pure'.

Agrippina
Latin, from the expression, meaning 'born feet first'.

Aida
Arabic, meaning 'reward' or 'present'.

Aidanne
(alt. Aidan, Aidenn)
Gaelic, meaning 'fire'.

Ailbhe
Irish, meaning 'noble' or 'bright'.

A

Aileen

(alt. Aelinn, Aleen, Aline, Alline, Eileen)

Gaelic variant of Helen, meaning 'light'.

Ailith

(alt. Ailish)

Old English, meaning 'seasoned warrior'.

Ailsa

Scottish, meaning 'pledge from God', as well as the name of a Scottish island, Ailsa Craig.

Aimee

(alt. Aimie, Amie)

French form of Amy, meaning 'beloved'.

Aina

Scandinavian, meaning 'forever'.

Aine

(alt. Aino)

Celtic, meaning 'happiness'.

Ainsley

Scottish and Gaelic, meaning 'one's own meadow'.

Aisha

(alt. Aeysha)

Arabic, meaning 'woman'; as well as Swahili, meaning 'life'.

Aishwarya

Variant of the Arabic Aisha, meaning 'woman'.

Aislinn

(alt. Aislin, Aisling, Aislyn, Alene, Allene)

Irish Gaelic, meaning 'dream'.

Aiyanna

(alt. Aiyana)

Native American, meaning 'forever flowering'.

Aja

Hindi, meaning 'goat'.

Aka

(alt. Akah, Akkah)

Maori, meaning 'loving one'.

Akela

(alt. Akilah)

Hawaiian, meaning 'noble'.

Akilina

Greek or Russian, meaning 'eagle'.

Akiva

Hebrew, meaning 'protect and shelter'.

Alaina

(alt. Alane, Alani, Alayna, Aleena)

Feminine of Alan, from the Gaelic for 'rock' or 'comely'.

Alana

(alt. Alanna, Alannah)

Variant of Alaina, meaning 'rock' or 'comely'.

Alanis

(alt. Alarice)

Variant of Alaina, meaning 'rock' or 'comely'.

Alba

Latin, meaning 'white'. Also the Gaelic word for 'Scotland'.

Alberta

(alt. Albertha, Albertine)

Feminine of Albert, from the Old German for 'noble, bright, famous'.

Albina

Latin, meaning 'white' or 'fair'.

Alda

German, meaning 'old' or 'prosperous'.

Aldis

English, meaning 'battle-seasoned'.

Aleah

Arabic, meaning 'high'; also Persian, meaning 'one of God's beings'.

Aleta

(alt. Aletha)

Greek, meaning 'footloose'.

Alethea

(alt. Aletheia)

Greek, meaning 'truth'.

Alex

(alt. Alexa, Alexi, Alexia, Alexina)

Shortened version of Alexandra, meaning 'man's defender'.

Alexandra

(alt. Alejandra, Alejhandra, Aleksandra, Alessandra, Alexandria)

Feminine of Alexander, from the Greek interpretation of 'man's defender'.

A

Alexis
(alt. Alexus, Alexys)
Greek, meaning 'helper'.

Aleydis
Variant of Alice, meaning 'noble' or 'nobility'.

Alfreda
Old English, meaning 'elf power'.

Ali
(alt. Allie, Ally)
Shortened version of Alexandra, Aliyah or Alice.

Alibeth
Variant of Elizabeth, meaning 'consecrated to God'.

Alice
(alt. Alize, Alyce, Alys, Alyse)
English, meaning 'noble' or 'nobility'.

Alicia
(alt. Ahlicia, Alecia, Alesia, Alessia, Alizia, Alycia, Alysia)
Variant of Alice, meaning 'nobility'.

Alida
(alt. Aleida)
Latin, meaning 'small winged one'.

Alienor
(alt. Aliana)
Variant of Eleanor, from the Greek for 'light'.

Aliki
(alt. Alika)
Variant of Alice, meaning 'nobility'.

Alima
Arabic, meaning 'cultured'.

Alina
(alt. Alena)
Slavic variation of Helen, meaning 'light'.

Alisha
(alt. Alesha, Alysha)
Variant of Alice, meaning 'nobility'.

Alison
(alt. Allison, Allisyn, Allyson, Alyson)
Variant of Alice, meaning 'nobility'.

Alissa
(alt. Alessa, Alise)

Greek, meaning 'pretty'.

Alivia

Variant of Olivia, meaning 'olive tree'.

Aliya
(alt. Aaliyah, Aleah, Alia, Aliah, Aliyah)

Arabic, meaning 'exalted' or 'sublime'.

Alla

Variant of Ella or Alexandra. Also a possible reference to Allah.

Allegra

Italian, meaning 'joyous'.

Allura

French, from the word for entice, meaning 'the power of attraction'.

Allyn

Feminine of Alan, meaning 'peaceful'.

Alma

Three possible origins: Latin for 'giving nurture', Italian for 'soul' and Arabic for 'learned'.

Almeda
(alt. Almeta)

Latin, meaning 'ambitious'.

Almera
(alt. Almira)

Feminine of Elmer, from the Arabic for 'aristocratic' and the Old English meaning 'noble'.

Alohi

Variant of the Hawaiian greeting Aloha, meaning 'love and affection'.

Alona

Hebrew, meaning 'oak tree'.

Alora

Variant of Alona, meaning 'oak tree'.

Alpha

The first letter of the Greek alphabet, usually given to a firstborn daughter.

Alta

Latin, meaning 'elevated'.

Altagracia

Spanish, meaning 'grace'.

Althea

(alt. Altea, Altha)

Greek, meaning 'healing power'.

Alva

Spanish, meaning 'blonde' or 'fair skinned'.

Alvena

(alt. Alvina)

English, meaning 'noble friend'.

Alvia

(alt. Alyvia)

Variant of Olivia, meaning 'olive tree' or Elvira from the ancient Spanish city.

Alyssa

(alt. Alisa, Allyssa, Alysa)

Greek, meaning 'rational'.

Amabel

Variant of Annabel, meaning 'grace and beauty'.

Amadea

Feminine of Amadeus, meaning 'God's'.

Amalia

Variant of Emilia, Latin, meaning 'rival, eager'.

Amana

Hebrew, meaning 'loyal and true'.

Amanda

Latin, meaning 'much loved'.

Amandine

Variant of Amanda, meaning 'much loved'.

Amara

(alt. Amani)

Greek, meaning 'lovely forever'.

Amarantha

Contraction of Amanda and Samantha, meaning 'much loved listener'.

Amaris

(alt. Amari, Amasa, Amata, Amaya)

Hebrew, meaning 'pledged by God'.

Amaryllis

Greek, meaning 'fresh'. Also a flower by the same name.

Amber

French, from the word for the semi-precious stone of the same name.

Amberly

Contraction of Amber and Leigh, meaning 'stone' and 'meadow'.

Amberlynn

Contraction of Amber and Lynn, meaning 'stone' and 'waterfall'.

Amboree
(alt. Amber, Ambree)

American, meaning 'precocious'.

Amelia
(alt. Aemilia)

Greek, meaning 'industrious'.

Amelie
(alt. Amalie)

French form of Amelia, meaning 'industrious'.

America

From the country of the same name.

Ameris

Variant of Amaryllis, meaning 'fresh'.

Amethyst

Greek, from the word for the precious stone of the same name.

Amina

Arabic, meaning 'honest and trustworthy'.

Amira
(alt. Amiya, Amiyah)

Arabic, meaning 'a high-born girl'.

Amity

Latin, meaning 'friendship and harmony'.

Amory

Variant of the Spanish name Amor, meaning 'love'.

Amy
(alt. Aimee, Amee, Ami, Amie, Ammie)

Latin, meaning 'beloved'.

Amya

Variant of Amy, meaning 'beloved'.

Ana-Lisa

Contraction of Anna and Lisa, meaning 'grace' or 'consecrated to God'.

Anafa

Hebrew, meaning 'heron'.

Ananda

Hindi, meaning 'bliss'.

Anastasia

(alt. Athanasia)

Greek, meaning 'resurrection'.

Anatolia

From the eastern Greek town of the same name.

Andelyn

Contraction of the feminine for Andrew and Lynn, meaning 'strong waterfall'.

Andrea

(alt. Andreia, Andria)

Feminine of Andrew, from the Greek term for 'a man's woman'.

Andrine

Variant of Andrea, meaning 'a man's woman'.

Andromeda

Greek, meaning 'leader of men'. From the heroine of a Greek legend.

Anemone

Greek, meaning 'breath'. Also from the flower.

Angela

(alt. Angel, Angeles, Angelia Angelle, Angie)

Greek, meaning 'messenger from God' or 'angel'.

Angelica

(alt. Angelina, Angeline, Angelique, Angelise, Angelita, Anjelica, Anjelina)

Latin, meaning 'angelic'.

Anise

(alt. Anisa, Anissa)

French, from the licorice flavoured plant of the same name.

Anita

(alt. Anitra)

Variant of Ann, meaning 'grace'.

Ann

(alt. Anne, Annie)

Derived from Hannah, meaning 'grace'.

227

Anna
(alt. Ana, Anne)
Derived from Hannah,
meaning 'grace'.

Annabel
*(alt. Anabel, Anabelle, Annabell,
Annabella, Annabelle)*
Contraction of Anna and Belle,
meaning 'grace' and 'beauty'.

Annalise
*(alt. Annalee, Annaliese,
Annalisa, Anneli, Annelie,
Annelies, Annelise)*
Contraction of Anna and Lise,
meaning 'grace' and 'pledged
to God'.

Annemarie
*(alt. Annamae, Annamarie,
Annelle, Annmarie)*
Contraction of Anna and Mary,
meaning 'grace' and 'star of the
sea'.

Annette
(alt. Annetta)
Derived from Hannah, Hebrew,
meaning 'grace'.

Annis
Greek, meaning 'finished or
completed'.

Annora
Latin, meaning 'honour'.

Anoushka
(alt. Anousha)
Russian variant of Ann,
meaning 'grace'.

Ansley
English, meaning 'the awesome
one's meadow'.

Anthea
(alt. Anthi)
Greek, meaning 'flowerlike'.

Antigone
In Greek mythology, Antigone
was the daughter of Oedipus.

Antoinette
*(alt. Anonetta, Antonette,
Antonietta)*
Both a variation of Ann and the
feminine of Anthony, meaning
'invaluable grace'.

Antonia
(alt. Antonella, Antonina)
Latin, meaning 'invaluable'.

Anwen
Welsh, meaning 'very fair'.

Anya
(alt. Aniya, Aniyah, Aniylah, Anja)

Russian, meaning 'grace'.

Aoife
Gaelic, meaning 'beautiful joy'.

Apollonia
Feminine of Apollo, the Greek god of the sun.

Apple
From the name of the fruit.

April
(alt. Avril)

Latin, meaning 'opening up'. Also the name of the month.

Aquilina
(alt. Aqua, Aquila)

Spanish, meaning 'like an eagle'.

Ara
Arabic, meaning 'brings rain'.

Arabella
Latin, meaning 'answered prayer'.

Araceli
(alt. Aracely)

Spanish, meaning 'altar of Heaven'.

Araylia
(alt. Araelea)

Latin, meaning 'golden'.

Arcadia
Greek, meaning 'paradise'.

Ardelle
(alt. Ardell, Ardella)

Latin, meaning 'burning with enthusiasm'.

Arden
(alt. Ardis, Ardith)

Latin, meaning 'burning with enthusiasm'.

Arella
(alt. Areli, Arely)

Hebrew, meaning 'angel'.

Aretha
Greek, meaning 'woman of virtue'.

Aria
(alt. Ariah)

Italian, meaning 'melody'.

A

Ariadne

Greek and Latin, meaning 'the very holy one'. In Greek mythology, Ariadne was the daughter of King Minos.

Ariana
(alt. Ariane, Arianna, Arienne)
Welsh, meaning 'silver'.

Ariel
(alt. Ariela, Ariella, Arielle)
Hebrew, meaning 'lioness of God'. One of the archangels.

Arlene
(alt. Arleen, Arlie, Arline, Arly)
Gaelic, meaning 'pledge'.

Armida

Latin, meaning 'little armed one'.

Artemisia
(alt. Artemis)
Greek and Spanish, meaning 'perfect'.

Artie
(alt. Arti)
Shortened form of Artemisia, meaning 'perfect'.

Ashanti

From the geographical area in Ghana, Africa.

Ashby

English, meaning 'ash tree farm'. Also name of place in Leicestershire.

Ashley
(alt. Ashely, Ashlee, Ashleigh, Ashli, Ashlie, Ashly)
English, meaning 'ash tree meadow'.

Ashlynn
(alt. Ashlyn)
Irish Gaelic, meaning 'dream'.

Ashton
(alt. Ashtyn)
Old English, meaning 'ash tree town'. From the place name.

Asia

From the name of the continent.

Asma
(alt. Asmara)
Arabic, meaning 'high-standing'.

Aspen
(alt. Aspynn)

From the name of the tree. Also name of a city in the US.

Assumpta
(alt. Assunta)

Italian, meaning 'raised up'.

Asta
(alt. Asteria, Astor, Astoria)

Greek or Latin, meaning 'star-like'.

Astrid

Old Norse, meaning 'beautiful like a God'.

Atara

Hebrew, meaning 'diadem'.

Athena
(alt. Athenais)

Greek, meaning 'wise'. From the Greek goddess of wisdom.

Aubrey
(alt. Aubree, Aubriana, Aubrie)

French, meaning 'elf ruler'.

Audrey
(alt. Audra, Audrie, Audrina, Audry, Autry)

English, meaning 'noble strength'.

Audrina

Variant of Audrey, meaning 'noble strength'.

Augusta
(alt. August, Augustine)

Latin, meaning 'worthy of respect'.

Aura
(alt. Aurea)

Greek or Latin, meaning either 'soft breeze' or 'gold'.

Popular French names

Belle	Lilou
Camille	Maelys
Colette	Romane
Fleur	Sabine
Léa	Yvette

Aurelia
(alt. Aurelie)
Latin, meaning 'gold'.

Aurora
(alt. Aurore)
Latin, meaning 'dawn'. In Roman mythology, Aurora was the goddess of sunrise.

Austine
(alt. Austen, Austin)
Latin, meaning 'worthy of respect'.

Autumn
From the name of the season

Ava
(alt. Avia, Avie)
Latin, meaning 'like a bird'.

Avalon
(alt. Avalyn, Aveline)
Celtic, meaning 'island of apples'.

Axelle
Greek, meaning 'father of peace'.

Aya
(alt. Ayah)
Hebrew, meaning 'bird'.

Ayanna
(alt. Ayana)
American, meaning 'grace'.

Ayesha
(alt. Aisha, Aysha)
Persian, meaning 'small one'.

Azalea
Latin, meaning 'dry earth'.

Azalia
Hebrew, meaning 'aided by God'.

Aziza
Hebrew, meaning 'mighty', or Arabic, meaning 'precious'.

Azure
(alt. Azaria)
French, meaning 'sky-blue'.

Girls' names

Babette

French version of Barbara, from the Greek word meaning 'foreign'.

Badia

(alt. Badiyn, Badea)

Arabic, meaning 'elegant'.

Bailey

(alt. Baeli, Bailee)

English, meaning 'law enforcer'.

Bambi

Shortened version of the Italian Bambina, meaning 'child'.

Barbara

(alt. Barb, Barbie, Barbra)

Greek, meaning 'foreign'.

Basma

Arabic, meaning 'smile'.

Bathsheba

Hebrew, meaning 'daughter of the oath'.

Bay

(alt. Baya)

From the plant or geographical name.

Beata

Latin, meaning 'blessed'.

Beatrice

(alt. Beatrix, Beatriz, Bellatrix, Betrys)

Latin, meaning 'bringer of gladness'.

Literary names

Alice (*Alice in Wonderland*, Lewis Carroll)
Bella (Twilight novels, Stephenie Meyer)
Charlotte (*Charlotte's Web*, E. B. White)
Emma (*Madame Bovary*, Gustave Flaubert)
Esther (*Bleak House*, Charles Dickens)
Iris (*The Blind Assassin*, Margaret Atwood)
Hermione (Harry Potter series, J. K. Rowling)
Lyra (His Dark Materials series, Phillip Pullman)
Matilda (*Matilda*, Roald Dahl)
Shirley (*Shirley*, Charlotte Brontë)
Wendy (*Peter Pan*, J. M. Barrie)

Becky
(alt. Beccie, Beccy, Beckie)
Shortened form of Rebecca,
Hebrew meaning 'joined'.

Bee
Shortened form of Beatrice,
meaning 'bringer of gladness'.

Belinda
(alt. Belen, Belina)
Contraction of Belle and Linda,
meaning 'beautiful'.

Bell
Shortened form of Isabel,
meaning 'pledged to God'.

Bella
Latin, meaning 'beautiful'.

Belle
French, meaning 'beautiful'.

Belva
Latin, meaning 'beautiful view'.

Bénédicta
Latin, the feminine of Benedict,
meaning 'blessed'.

Benita
(alt. Bernita)
Spanish, meaning 'blessed'.

234

Bennie

Shortened version of Bénédicta and Benita, meaning 'blessed'.

Berit
(alt. Beret)

Scandinavian, meaning 'splendid' or 'gorgeous'.

Bernadette

French, meaning 'courageous'.

Bernadine

French, meaning 'courageous'.

Bernice
(alt. Berenice, Berniece, Burnice)

Greek, meaning 'she who brings victory'.

Bertha
(alt. Berta, Berthe, Bertie)

German, meaning 'bright'.

Beryl

Greek, meaning 'pale green gemstone'.

Bess
(alt. Bessie)

Shortened form of Elizabeth, meaning 'consecrated to God'.

Beth

Hebrew, meaning 'house'. Also shortened form of Elizabeth, meaning 'consecrated to God'.

Bethany
(alt. Bethan)

Hebrew, referring to a geographical location.

Bethel

Hebrew, meaning 'house of God'.

Bettina

Spanish version of Elizabeth, meaning 'consecrated to God'.

Betty
(alt. Betsy, Bette, Bettie, Bettye)

Shortened version of Elizabeth, meaning 'consecrated to God'.

Beulah

Hebrew, meaning 'married'.

Beverly
(alt. Beverlee, Beverley)

English, meaning 'beaver stream'.

Bevin

Celtic, meaning 'fair lady'.

B

Beyoncé

American, made popular by the singer.

Bianca

(alt. Blanca)

Italian, meaning 'white'.

Bibiana

Greek, meaning 'alive'.

Bijou

French, meaning 'jewel'.

Billie

(alt. Bill, Billy, Billye)

Shortened version of Wilhelmina, meaning 'determined'.

Bina

Hebrew, meaning 'knowledge'.

Birgit

(alt. Birgitta)

Norwegian, meaning 'splendid'.

Blaer

Icelandic, meaning 'light breeze'.

Blair

Scottish Gaelic, meaning 'flat, plain area'.

Blake

(alt. Blakely, Blakelyn)

English, meaning either 'pale-skinned' or 'dark'.

Blanche

(alt. Blanch)

French, meaning 'white or pale'.

Blithe

English, meaning 'joyous'.

Blodwen

Welsh, meaning 'white flower'.

Blossom

English, meaning 'flowerlike'.

Blythe

(alt. Bly)

English, meaning 'happy and carefree'.

Bobbi

(alt. Bobbie, Bobby)

Shortened version of Roberta, meaning 'bright fame'.

Bonamy
(alt. Bomani, Bonamia, Bonamea)

French, meaning 'close friend'.

Bonita
Spanish, meaning 'pretty'.

Bonnie
(alt. Bonny)

Scottish, meaning 'fair of face'.

Brandy
(alt. Brandee, Brandi, Brandie)

From the name of the liquor.

Branwen
Welsh, meaning 'a white crow'.

Brea
(alt. Bree, Bria)

Shortened form of Brianna, meaning 'strong'.

Brenda
Old Norse, meaning 'sword'.

Brianna
(alt. Breana, Breanna, Breanne)

Irish Gaelic, meaning 'strong'.

Bridget
(alt. Bridgett, Bridgette, Brigette, Brigid, Brigitta, Brigitte)

Irish Gaelic, meaning 'strength and power'.

Brier
French, meaning 'heather'.

Brit
(alt. Britt, Britta)

Celtic, meaning 'spotted' or 'freckled'.

Britannia
Latin, meaning 'Britain'.

Biblical names

Abigail
Delilah
Eve
Hannah
Mary
Naomi
Rebecca
Ruth
Sarah
Salome

B

Brittany
(alt. Britany, Britney, Britni, Brittani, Brittanie, Brittney, Brittni, Brittny)

Latin, meaning 'from England'.

Bronwyn
(alt. Bronwen)

Welsh, meaning 'fair breast'.

Brooke
(alt. Brook)

English, meaning 'small stream'.

Brooklyn
(alt. Brooklynn)

From the name of a New York borough.

Brunhilda

German, meaning 'armour-wearing fighting maid'.

Bryn
(alt. Brynn)

Welsh, meaning 'mount'.

Bryony
(alt. Briony)

From the name of a European vine.

Buffy

American alternative of Elizabeth, meaning 'consecrated to God'.

Popular Spanish names

Ana
Carla
Carmen
Daniela
Elena
Maria
Marina
Natalia
Sara
Sofia

C Girls' names

Cadence

Latin, meaning 'with rhythm'.

Cadew

French, meaning 'gift'.

Cai

Vietnamese, meaning 'feminine'.

Caitlin

(alt. Cadyn, Caitlann, Caitlyn, Caitlynn)

Greek, meaning 'pure'.

Calandra

Greek, meaning 'lark'.

Calantha

(alt. Calanthe)

Greek, meaning 'lovely flower'.

Caledonia

Latin, meaning 'from Scotland'.

Calia

American, meaning 'renowned beauty'.

Calla

Greek, meaning 'beautiful'.

Callie

(alt. Caleigh, Cali, Calleigh, Cally)

Greek, meaning 'beauty'.

Calliope

Greek, meaning 'beautiful voice'. From the muse of epic poetry in Greek mythology.

Callista

(alt. Callisto)

Greek, meaning 'most beautiful'.

239

Camas

Native American, from the root and bulb of the same name.

Cambria

Welsh, from the alternative name for Wales.

Camden
(alt. Camdyn)

English, meaning 'winding valley'.

Cameo

Italian, meaning 'skin'.

Cameron
(alt. Camryn)

Scottish Gaelic, meaning 'bent nose'.

Camilla
(alt. Camelia, Camellia, Camila, Camillia)

Latin, meaning 'spiritual serving girl'.

Camille

Latin, meaning 'spiritual serving girl'.

Candace
(alt. Candice, Candis)

Latin, meaning 'brilliant white'.

Candida

Latin, meaning 'white'.

Candra

Latin, meaning 'glowing'.

Candy
(alt. Candi)

Shortened form of Candace, meaning 'brilliant white'.

Canei

Greek, meaning 'pure'.

Caoimhe

Celtic, meaning 'gentleness'.

Caprice

Italian, meaning 'ruled by whim'.

Cara

Latin, meaning 'darling'.

Caren
(alt. Carin, Caron, Caryn)

Greek, meaning 'pure'.

Carey

(alt. Cari, Carie, Carri, Carrie, Cary)

Welsh, meaning 'near the castle'.

Carina

(alt. Corina)

Italian, meaning 'dearest little one'.

Carissa

(alt. Carisa)

Greek, meaning 'grace'.

Carla

(alt. Charla)

Feminine of the Old Norse Carl, meaning 'free man'.

Carlin

(alt. Carleen, Carlene)

Gaelic, meaning 'little champion'.

Carlotta

(alt. Carlota)

Italian form of Charlotte, meaning 'little and feminine'.

Carly

(alt. Carlee, Carley, Carli, Carlie)

Feminine of the German Charles, meaning 'free man'.

Carmel

(alt. Carmela, Carmelita, Carmella)

Hebrew, meaning 'garden'.

Carmen

(alt. Carma, Carmina)

Latin, meaning 'song'.

Carol

(alt. Carole, Carrol, Carroll, Caryl)

Shortened form of Caroline, meaning 'man'.

Caroline

(alt. Carolann, Carolina, Carolyn, Carolynn)

German, meaning 'man'.

Carrington

English, meaning 'Charles's town'.

Carys

(alt. Cerys)

Welsh, meaning 'love'.

Casey

Irish Gaelic, meaning 'watchful'.

Saints' names

Agatha
Agnes
Barbara
Cecilia
Genevieve
Louise
Matilda
Seraphina
Tatiana
Teresa
Vivian

Cassandra
(alt. Casandra, Cassandre)
Greek, meaning 'one who prophesies doom'.

Cassia
(alt. Casia, Casie, Cassie)
Greek, meaning 'cinnamon'.

Cassidy
Irish, meaning 'clever'.

Cassiopeia
(alt. Cassiopia, Cassiopea)
Greek, from the constellation and the Greek myth.

Catalina
(alt. Catarina, Caterina)
Spanish version of Catherine, meaning 'pure'.

Catherine
(alt. Catharine, Cathrine, Cathryn)
Greek, meaning 'pure'.

Cathleen
Irish version of Catherine, meaning 'pure'.

Cathy
(alt. Cathey, Cathi, Cathie)
Shortened form of Catherine, meaning 'pure'.

Caty
(alt. Caddie, Caitee, Caitie Cate, Catie)
Shortened form of Catherine, meaning 'pure'.

Cayley
(alt. Cayla, Caylee, Caylen)
American, meaning 'pure'.

Cecile
(alt. Cecilie)
Latin, meaning 'blind one'.

Cecilia
(alt. Cecelia, Cecily, Cicely, Cicily)
Latin, meaning 'blind one'.

Celena
Greek, meaning 'goddess of the moon'.

Celeste
(alt. Celestina, Celestine)
Latin, meaning 'heavenly'.

Celine
(alt. Celia, Celina)
French version of Celeste, meaning 'heavenly'.

Cerise
French, meaning 'cherry'.

Chanah
Hebrew, meaning 'grace'.

Chandler
(alt. Chandell)
English, meaning 'candle maker'.

Chandra
(alt. Chanda, Chandry)
Sanskrit, meaning 'like the moon'.

Chanel
(alt. Chanelle)
French, meaning 'pipe'. Most often associated with the designer of the same name.

Chantal
(alt. Chantel, Chantelle, Chantilly)
French, meaning 'stony spot'.

Chardonnay
French, from the wine variety of the same name.

Charis
(alt. Charissa, Charisse)
Greek, meaning 'grace'.

Charity
Latin, meaning 'brotherly love'.

Charlene
(alt. Charleen, Charline)
German, meaning 'man'.

Charlie
(alt. Charlee, Charley, Charlize, Charly)
Shortened form of Charlotte, meaning 'little and feminine'.

Charlotte
(alt. Charnette, Charolette)
French, meaning 'little and feminine'.

Charmaine
Latin, meaning 'clan'.

Charnelle
(alt. Charnell, Charnel, Charnele)
American, meaning 'sparkles'.

Chastity
Latin, meaning 'purity'.

Chava
(alt. Chaya)
Hebrew, meaning 'beloved'.

Chelsea
(alt. Chelsee, Chelsey, Chelsi, Chelsie)
English, meaning 'port or landing place'.

Cher
French, meaning 'beloved'. Most often associated with the singer of the same name.

Cherie
(alt. Cheri, Cherise)
French, meaning 'dear'.

Cherish
(alt. Cherith)
English, meaning 'to treasure'.

Chermona
Hebrew, meaning 'sacred mountain'.

Cherry
(alt. Cherri)
French, meaning 'cherry fruit'.

TV personality names

Alex (Jones)
Alesha (Dixon)
Caroline (Flack)
Cheryl (Cole)
Christine (Bleakley)
Davina (McCall)
Fearne (Cotton)
Holly (Willoughby)
Kirsty (Alsopp)
Lauren (Laverne)
Myleene (Klass)
Tess (Daly)

Cheryl
(alt. Cheryle)
English, meaning 'little and womanly'.

Chesney
English, meaning 'place to camp'.

Cheyenne
(alt. Cheyanne)
Native American, from the tribe of the same name.

Chiara
(alt. Ceara, Chiarina, Ciara)
Italian, meaning 'light'.

China
From the country of the same name.

Chiquita
Spanish, meaning 'little one'.

Chloe
(alt. Cloe)
Greek, meaning 'pale green shoot'.

Chloris
Greek, meaning 'pale'.

Chris
(alt. Chrissy, Christa, Christie, Christy, Crissy, Cristy)
Shortened form of Christina, meaning 'anointed Christian'.

Christabel
Latin and French, meaning 'fair Christian'. The title of a poem by Coleridge.

Christina
(alt. Christiana, Cristina)
Greek, meaning 'anointed Christian'.

Christine
(alt. Christeen, Christene, Christiane, Christin)
Greek, meaning 'anointed Christian'.

Chuma
Aramaic, meaning 'warmth'.

Ciara
Irish, meaning 'dark beauty'.

Cierra
(alt. Ciera)
Irish, meaning 'black'.

Cinderella

French, meaning 'little ash-girl'. Most often associated with the fairytale.

Cindy

(alt. Cinda, Cindi, Cyndi)

Shortened form of Cynthia, meaning 'goddess from the mountain'.

Cinnamon

Greek, from the spice of the same name.

Citlali

(alt. Citlalli)

Aztec, meaning 'star'.

Citrine

Latin, from the gemstone of the same name.

Claire

(alt. Clare)

Latin, meaning 'bright'.

Clara

(alt. Claira)

Latin, meaning 'bright'.

Clarabelle

(alt. Claribel)

Contraction of Clara and Isobel, meaning 'bright' and 'consecrated to God'.

Clarissa

(alt. Clarice, Clarisse)

Variation of Claire, meaning 'bright'.

Clarity

Latin, meaning 'lucid'.

Claudette

Latin, meaning 'lame'.

Claudia

(alt. Claudie, Claudine)

Latin, meaning 'lame'.

Clematis

Greek, meaning 'vine'.

Clementine

(alt. Clemency, Clementina, Clemmie)

Latin, meaning 'mild and merciful'.

Cleopatra

Greek, meaning 'her father's renown'. Most often associated with the Egyptian queen.

C

Clio
(alt. *Cleo, Cliona*)
Greek, from the muse of history of the same name.

Clodagh
Irish, meaning 'river'.

Clotilda
(alt. *Clothilda, Clothilde, Clotilde*)
German, meaning 'renowned battle'.

Clover
English, from the flower of the same name.

Coco
Spanish, meaning 'help'.

Cody
English, meaning 'pillow'.

Colleen
(alt. *Coleen*)
Irish Gaelic, meaning 'girl'.

Collette
(alt. *Colette*)
Greek and French, meaning 'people of victory'.

Connie
Latin, meaning 'steadfast'.

Constance
(alt. *Constanza*)
Latin, meaning 'steadfast'.

Consuelo
(alt. *Consuela*)
Spanish, meaning 'comfort'.

Cora
Greek, meaning 'maiden'.

Coral
(alt. *Coralie, Coraline, Corelia, Corene*)
Latin, from the marine life of the same name.

Corazon
Spanish, meaning 'heart'.

Cordelia
(alt. *Cordia, Cordie*)
Latin, meaning 'heart'.

Corey
(alt. *Cori, Corrie, Cory*)
Irish Gaelic, meaning 'the hollow'.

Corin
(alt. Corine)
Latin, meaning 'spear'.

Corinne
(alt. Corinna, Corrine)
French version of Cora, meaning 'maiden'.

Corliss
English, meaning 'cheery'.

Cornelia
Latin, meaning 'like a horn'.

Cosette
French, meaning 'people of victory'. Also the heroine in *Les Misérables*.

Cosima
(alt. Cosmina)
Greek, meaning 'order'.

Courtney
(alt. Cortney)
English, meaning 'court-dweller'.

Creola
French, meaning 'American-born, English descent'.

Crescent
French, meaning 'increasing'.

Cressida
From the heroine in Greek mythology of the same name.

Crystal
(alt. Christal, Chrystal, Cristal)
Greek, meaning 'ice'.

Csilla
Hungarian, meaning 'defences'.

Cyd
Shortened form of Sidney, meaning 'wide island'.

Cynara
Greek, meaning 'thistly plant'.

Cynthia
Greek, meaning 'goddess from the mountain'.

Cyra
Persian, meaning 'sun'.

Cyrilla
Latin, meaning 'lordly'.

Girls' names

Dacey

Irish Gaelic, meaning 'from the south'.

Dada

Nigerian, meaning 'curly haired'.

Daelan

English, meaning 'aware'.

Dagmar

German, meaning 'day's glory'.

Dagny

Nordic, meaning 'new day'.

Dahlia

Scandinavian, from the flower of the same name.

Dai

Japanese, meaning 'great'.

Daisy
(alt. Dasia)

English, meaning 'eye of the day'. Also the flower.

Dakota

Native American, meaning 'allies'.

Dalia
(alt. Dalila)

Hebrew, meaning 'delicate branch'.

Dallas

Scottish Gaelic, from the village of the same name. Also a city in the US.

Damaris

Greek, meaning 'calf'.

Damica

(alt. Damika)

French, meaning 'friendly'.

Damita

Spanish, meaning 'little noblewoman'.

Dana

(alt. Dania, Danna, Dayna)

English, meaning 'from Denmark'.

Danae

Greek, from the mythological heroine of the same name.

Danica

(alt. Danika)

Latin, meaning 'from Denmark'.

Danielle

(alt. Danelle, Daniela, Daniella, Danila, Danyelle)

The feminine form of the Hebrew Daniel, meaning 'God is my judge'.

Danita

English, meaning 'God will judge'.

Daphne

(alt. Dafne, Daphna)

Greek, meaning 'laurel tree'.

Dara

Hebrew and Persian, meaning 'wisdom'.

Darby

(alt. Darbi, Darbie)

Irish, meaning 'park with deer'.

Darcie

(alt. Darci, Darcy)

Irish Gaelic, meaning 'dark'.

Daria

Greek, meaning 'rich'.

Darla

English, meaning 'darling'.

Darlene

(alt. Darleen, Darline)

American, meaning 'darling'.

Darva

Slavic, meaning 'honeybee'.

Daryl
(alt. Darryl)
English, originally used as a surname. Often associated with the actress Daryl Hannah.

Davina
Hebrew, meaning 'loved one'. Best known for the TV presenter Davina McCall.

Dawn
(alt. Dawna)
English, meaning 'the dawn'.

Daya
Hebrew, meaning 'bird of prey'.

Deanna
(alt. Dayana, Deana, Deanna, Deanne)
English, meaning 'valley'.

Debbie
(alt. Debbi, Debby, Debi)
Shortened form of Deborah, meaning 'bee'.

Deborah
(alt. Debbra, Debora, Debra, Debrah)
Hebrew, meaning 'bee'.

December
Latin, meaning 'tenth month'.

Decima
(alt. Decia)
Latin, meaning 'tenth'.

Dee
Welsh, meaning 'swarthy'.

Deidre
(alt. Deidra, Deirdre)
Irish, meaning 'raging woman'.

Deja
(alt. Dejah)
French, meaning 'already'.

Delaney
Irish Gaelic, meaning 'offspring of the challenger'.

Delia
Greek, meaning 'from Delos'.

Delilah
(alt. Delina)
Hebrew, meaning 'seductive'.

Della
(alt. Dell)
Shortened form of Adele, meaning 'nobility'.

Delores
(alt. Deloris)
Spanish, meaning 'sorrows'.

Delphine
(alt. Delpha, Delphia, Delphina, Delphinia)
Greek, meaning 'dolphin'.

Delta
Greek, meaning 'fourth child'.

Demetria
(alt. Demetrice, Dimitria)
Greek, from the mythological heroine of the same name.

Demi
French, meaning 'half'. Best known for the actress Demi Moore.

Dena
(alt. Deena)
English, meaning 'from the valley'.

Denise
(alt. Denice, Denisa, Denisse)
French, meaning 'follower of Dionysius'.

Derora
Hebrew, meaning 'stream'.

Desdemona
Greek, meaning 'wretchedness'.

Desiree
(alt. Desirae)
French, meaning 'much desired'.

Desma
Greek, meaning 'blinding oath'.

Destiny
(alt. Destany, Destinee, Destiney, Destini)
French, meaning 'fate'.

Deva
Hindi, meaning 'God-like'.

Devin
(alt. Devinne)
Irish Gaelic, meaning 'poet'.

Devon
English, from the county of the same name.

Diamond
English, meaning 'brilliant'.

Diana
(alt. Dian, Diane, Dianna, Dianne)
Roman, meaning 'divine'.

D

Uncommon three-syllable names

Cassandra
Dolores
Gloria
Harriet
Imogen
Jessamy
Julia
Marilyn
Miranda
Nigella

Diandra

Greek, meaning 'two males'.

Dilys

Welsh, meaning 'reliable'.

Dimona

Hebrew, meaning 'south'.

Dinah
(alt. Dina)

Hebrew, meaning 'justified'.

Dionne

Greek, from the mythological heroine of the same name.

Divine

Italian, meaning 'heavenly'.

Dixie

French, meaning 'tenth'.

Dodie

Hebrew, meaning 'well-loved'.

Dolly
(alt. Dollie)

Shortened form of Dorothy, meaning 'gift of God'.

Dolores
(alt. Doloris)

Spanish, meaning 'sorrows'.

Dominique
(alt. Domenica, Dominica, Domonique)

Latin, meaning 'Lord'.

Donata

Latin, meaning 'given'.

Donna
(alt. Dona, Donnie)

Italian, meaning 'lady'.

Dora

Greek, meaning 'gift'.

D

Dorcas
Greek, meaning 'gazelle'.

Doreen
(alt. Dorene, Dorine)
Irish Gaelic, meaning 'brooding'.

Doria
Greek, meaning 'of the sea'.

Doris
(alt. Dorris)
Greek, from the region of the same name.

Dorothy
(alt. Dorathy, Doretha, Dorotha, Dorothea, Dorthy)
Greek, meaning 'gift of God'.

Dorrit
(alt. Dorit)
Greek, meaning 'gift of God'.

Dory
(alt. Dori)
French, meaning 'gilded'.

Dottie
(alt. Dotty)
Shortened form of Dorothy, meaning 'gift of God'.

Dove
(alt. Dovie)
English, from the bird of the same name.

Drew
Greek, meaning 'masculine'.

Drusilla
(alt. Drucilla)
Latin, meaning 'of the Drusus clan'.

Dulcie
(alt. Dulce, Dulcia)
Latin, meaning 'sweet'.

Dusty
(alt. Dusti)
Old German, meaning 'brave warrior'. Often associated with the singer Dusty Springfield.

E Girls' names

Eadlin
(alt. Eadlinn, Eadlyn, Eadlen)
Anglo-Saxon, meaning 'royalty'.

Earla
English, meaning 'leader'.

Eartha
English, meaning 'earth'.

Easter
Egyptian, from the festival of the same name.

Ebba
English, meaning 'fortress of riches'.

Ebony
(alt. Eboni)
Latin, meaning 'deep black wood'.

Echo
Greek, meaning 'reflected sound'. From the mythological nymph of the same name.

Eda
(alt. Edda)
English, meaning 'wealthy and happy'.

Edelmira
Spanish, meaning 'admired for nobility'.

Eden
Hebrew, meaning 'pleasure'.

Edie
(alt. Eddie)
Shortened form of Eden, meaning 'pleasure'.

Edina

Scottish, meaning 'from Edinburgh'.

Edith

(alt. Edyth)

English, meaning 'prosperity through battle'.

Edna

Hebrew, meaning 'enjoyment'.

Edrea

English, meaning 'wealthy and powerful'.

Edris

(alt. Edriss, Edrys)

Anglo-Saxon, meaning 'prosperous ruler'.

Edwina

English, meaning 'wealthy friend'.

Effie

Greek, meaning 'pleasant speech'.

Eglantine

French, from the shrub of the same name.

Eibhlín

Irish Gaelic, meaning 'shining and brilliant'.

Eileen

Irish, meaning 'shining and brilliant'.

Ekaterina

(alt. Ekaterini)

Slavic, meaning 'pure'.

Elaine

(alt. Elaina, Elayne)

French, meaning 'bright, shining light'.

Elba

Italian, from the island of the same name.

Elberta

English, meaning 'highborn'.

Eldora

Spanish, meaning 'covered with gold'.

Eldoris

(alt. Eldoriss, Eldorys)

Greek, meaning 'woman of the sea'.

Eleanor

(alt. Elana, Elanor, Eleanora)

Greek, meaning 'light'.

E

Electra
(alt. Elektra)
Greek, meaning 'shining'. Also from the myth.

Elfrida
(alt. Elfrieda)
English, meaning 'elf power'.

Eliane
Hebrew, meaning 'Jehovah is God'.

Elise
French, meaning 'my vow to God'.

Elissa
(alt. Elisa)
French, meaning 'pledged to God'.

Eliza
(alt. Elisha)
Hebrew, meaning 'consecrated to God'.

Elizabeth
(alt. Elisabet, Elisabeth, Elizabella, Elizabelle, Elsbeth, Elspeth)
Hebrew, meaning 'consecrated to God'.

Elke
German, meaning 'nobility'.

Ella
German, meaning 'completely'.

Elle
(alt. Ellie)
French, meaning 'she'.

Ellema
(alt. Ellemah, Elema, Ellemma, Elemah)
African, meaning 'dairy farmer'.

Ellen
(alt. Elin, Eline, Ellyn)
Greek, meaning 'shining'.

Ellice
(alt. Elyse)
Greek, meaning 'the Lord is God'.

Elma
(alt. Elna)
Latin, meaning 'soul'.

Elmira
Arabic, meaning 'aristocratic lady'.

Elodie
French, meaning 'marsh flower'.

Eloise
(alt. Elois, Eloisa, Elouise)
French, meaning 'renowned in battle'.

257

Elsa
(alt. Else, Elsie)

Hebrew, meaning 'consecrated to God'.

Elva
Irish, meaning 'noble'.

Elvina
English, meaning 'noble friend'.

Elvira
(alt. Elvera)

Spanish, from the ancient city of the same name.

Ember
(alt. Embry)

English, meaning 'spark'.

Emeline
German, meaning 'industrious'.

Emerald
English, meaning 'green gemstone'.

Emery
(alt. Emory)

German, meaning 'ruler of work'.

Emiko
(alt. Emuko)

Japanese, meaning 'pretty child'.

Emilia
Latin, meaning 'rival, eager'.

Emily
(alt. Emalee, Emelie, Emely, Emilee, Emilie, Emlyn)

Latin, meaning 'rival, eager'.

Emma
German, meaning 'embraces everything'. The title character of Jane Austen's novel.

Emmanuelle
Hebrew, meaning 'God is among us'.

Emmeline
(alt. Emmelina)

German, meaning 'embraces everything'.

Emmy
(alt. Emi, Emme, Emmie)

German, meaning 'embraces everything'.

Ena
Shortened form of Georgina, meaning 'farmer'.

Enid
(alt. Eneida)

Welsh, meaning 'life spirit'.

E

Enola
Native American, meaning 'solitary'.

Enya
Irish Gaelic, meaning 'fire'.

Eranthe
Greek, meaning 'delicate like the spring'.

Erica
(alt. Ericka, Erika)
Scandinavian, meaning 'ruler forever'.

Erin
(alt. Eryn)
Irish Gaelic, meaning 'from the isle to the west'.

Eris
Greek, from the mythological heroine of the same name.

Erlinda
Hebrew, meaning 'spirited'.

Erma
German, meaning 'universal'.

Ermine
French, meaning 'weasel'.

Erna
English, meaning 'sincere'.

Ernestine
(alt. Ernestina)
English, meaning 'sincere'.

Esme
French, meaning 'esteemed'.

Esmeralda
Spanish, meaning 'emerald'.

Esperanza
Spanish, meaning 'hope'.

Estelle
(alt. Estela, Estell, Estella)
French, meaning 'star'.

Esther
(alt. Esta, Ester, Etha, Ethna, Ethne)
Persian, meaning 'star'.

Etinia
(alt. Eteniah, Etene, Eteniya)
Native American, meaning 'prosperous'.

Eternity
Latin, meaning 'forever'.

E

Ethel
(alt. Ethyl)
English, meaning 'noble'.

Etta
(alt. Etter, Ettie)
Shortened form of Henrietta, meaning 'ruler of the house'.

Eudora
Greek, meaning 'generous gift'.

Eugenia
(alt. Eugenie)
Greek, meaning 'well born'.

Eulalia
(alt. Eula, Eulah, Eulalie)
Greek, meaning 'sweet-speaking'.

Eunice
Greek, meaning 'victorious'.

Euphemia
Greek, meaning ' favourable speech'.

Eva
Hebrew, meaning 'life'.

Evadne
Greek, meaning 'pleasing one'.

Evangeline
(alt. Evangelina)
Greek, meaning 'good news'.

Evanthe
Greek, meaning 'good flower'.

Eve
(alt. Evie)
Hebrew, meaning 'life'. The first woman created by God in the Bible.

Evelina
(alt. Evelia)
German, meaning 'hazelnut'.

Evelyn
(alt. Evalyn, Evelin, Eveline, Evelyne)
German, meaning 'hazelnut'.

Everly
(alt. Everleigh, Everley)
English, meaning 'grazing meadow'.

Evette
French, meaning 'yew wood'.

Evonne
(alt. Evon)
French, meaning 'yew wood'.

E

F

Girls' names

Fabia
(alt. *Fabiana, Fabienne, Fabiola, Fabriana*)
Latin, meaning 'from the Fabian clan'.

Fabrizia
Italian, meaning 'works with hands'.

Fahari
Swahili, meaning 'splendour'.

Faith
English, meaning 'loyalty'.

Faiza
Arabic, meaning 'victorious'.

Fallon
Irish Gaelic, meaning 'descended from a ruler'.

Fanny
(alt. *Fannie*)
Latin, meaning 'from France'.

Farica
German, meaning 'peaceful ruler'.

Farrah
English, meaning 'lovely and pleasant'.

Fatima
Arabic, meaning 'baby's nurse'.

Faustine
Latin, meaning 'fortunate'.

Fawn
French, meaning 'young deer'.

Fay
(alt. Fae, Faye)
French, meaning 'fairy'.

Fayola
(alt. Fayolah, Fayeena)
African, meaning 'walks with honour'.

Felicia
(alt. Felecia, Felice, Felicita, Felisha)
Latin, meaning 'lucky and happy'.

Felicity
Latin, meaning 'fortunate'.

Fenella
Irish Gaelic, meaning 'white shoulder'.

Fenia
Scandinavian, from the mythological giantess of the same name.

Fern
(alt. Fearne, Ferne, Ferrin)
English, from the plant of the same name.

Fernanda
German, meaning 'peace and courage'.

Ffion
(alt. Fion)
Irish Gaelic, meaning 'fair and pale'.

Old name, new fashion?

Arabella
Clara
Clarissa
Dorothy
Evelyn
Hazel
Marjorie
Nora
Penelope
Rosamond

Fia

Italian, meaning 'flame'.

Fifi

Hebrew, meaning 'Jehovah increases'.

Filomena

Greek, meaning 'loved one'.

Finlay

(alt. Finley)

Irish Gaelic, meaning 'fair-headed courageous one'.

Finola

(alt. Fionnula)

Irish Gaelic, meaning 'fair shoulder'.

Fiona

Irish Gaelic, meaning 'fair and pale'.

Fiora

Irish Gaelic, meaning 'fair and pale'.

Fiorella

Italian, meaning 'little flower'.

Flanna

(alt. Flannery)

Irish Gaelic, meaning 'russet hair'.

Flavia

Latin, meaning 'yellow hair'.

Fleur

French, meaning 'flower'.

Flo

(alt. Florrie, Flossie, Floy)

Shortened form of Florence, meaning 'in bloom'.

Flora

Latin, meaning 'flower'.

Florence

(alt. Florencia, Florene, Florine)

Latin, meaning 'in bloom'. Also the Italian city.

Florida

Latin, meaning 'flowery'. Also a state in the US.

Fran

(alt. Frankie, Frannie)

Shortened form of Frances, meaning 'from France'.

F

Frances
(alt. Francine, Francis)
Latin, meaning 'from France'.

Francesca
(alt. Franchesca, Francisca)
Latin, meaning 'from France'.

Freda
(alt. Freeda, Freida, Frida, Frieda)
German, meaning 'peaceful'.

Frederica
German, meaning 'peaceful ruler'.

Fuchsia
German, from the flower of the same name.

Fumik
Japanese, meaning 'little friend'.

Names of poets

Amy (Lowell)
Anne (Sexton)
Carol Ann (Duffy)
Charlotte (Smith)
Emily (Dickinson)
Fleur (Adcock)
Gwyneth (Lewis)
Pam (Ayres)
Ruth (Padel)
Sylvia (Plath)
Wendy (Cope)

F

Girls' names

Gabby
(alt. Gabbi)
Shortened form of Gabrielle, meaning 'heroine of God'.

Gabrielle
(alt. Gabriel, Gabriela, Gabriella)
Hebrew, meaning 'heroine of God'.

Gadara
Armenian, meaning 'mountain's peak'.

Gaia
(alt. Gaea)
Greek, meaning 'the earth'.

Gail
(alt. Gale, Gayla, Gayle)
Hebrew, meaning 'my father rejoices'.

Gala
French, meaning 'festive merrymaking'.

Galiena
German, meaning 'high one'.

Galina
Russian, meaning 'shining brightly'.

Garnet
(alt. Garnett)
English, meaning 'red gemstone'.

Gay
(alt. Gaye)
French, meaning 'glad and lighthearted'.

Gaynor

Welsh, meaning 'white and smooth'.

Gemini

Greek, meaning 'twin'. One of the signs of the zodiac.

Gemma

Italian, meaning 'precious stone'.

Gene

Greek, meaning 'wellborn'.

Genesis

Greek, meaning 'beginning'.

Geneva

(alt. Genevra)

French, meaning 'juniper tree'.

Genevieve

German, meaning 'white wave'.

Genie

Shortened form of Genevieve, meaning 'white wave'.

Georgette

French, meaning 'farmer'.

Names from ancient Rome

Agnes
Cecilia
Chloris
Diana
Flavia
Lavinia
Octavia
Paula
Portia
Tatiana

Georgia

(alt. Georgiana, Georgianna, Georgie)

Latin, meaning 'farmer'.

Georgina

(alt. Georgene, Georgine, Giorgina)

Latin, meaning 'farmer'.

Geraldine

German, meaning 'spear ruler'.

Gerda

Nordic, meaning 'shelter'.

G

Geri
(alt. Gerri, Gerry)
Shortened form of Geraldine, meaning 'spear ruler'.

Germaine
French, meaning 'from Germany'.

Gertie
Shortened form of Gertrude, meaning 'strength of a spear'.

Gertrude
German, meaning 'strength of a spear'.

Ghislaine
French, meaning 'pledge'.

Gia
(alt. Ghia)
Italian, meaning 'God is gracious'.

Gianina
(alt. Giana)
Hebrew, meaning 'God's graciousness'.

Gigi
(alt. Giget)
Shortened form of Georgina, meaning 'farmer'.

Gilda
English, meaning 'gilded'.

Gilia
Hebrew, meaning 'joy of the Lord'.

Gillian
Latin, meaning 'youthful'.

Gina
(alt. Geena, Gena)
Shortened form of Regina, meaning 'queen'.

Ginger
Latin, from the root of the same name.

Ginny
Shortened form of Virginia, meaning 'virgin'.

Giovanna
Italian, meaning 'God is gracious'.

Giselle
(alt. Gisela, Gisele, Giselle, Gisselle)
German, meaning 'pledge'.

Famous artists

Barbara (Hepworth)
Bridget (Riley)
Louise (Bourgeois)
Tracey (Emin)
Yoko (Ono)

Gita
(alt. Geeta)
Sanskrit, meaning 'song'.

Giulia
(alt. Giuliana)
Italian, meaning 'youthful'.

Gladys
(alt. Gladyce)
Welsh, meaning 'lame'.

Glenda
Welsh, meaning 'fair and good'.

Glenna
(alt. Glennie)
Irish Gaelic, meaning 'glen'.

Glenys
Welsh, meaning 'riverbank'.

Gloria
(alt. Glory)
Latin, meaning 'glory'.

Glynda
(alt. Glinda)
Welsh, meaning 'fair'. The good witch in the *Wizard of Oz*.

Glynis
Welsh, meaning 'small glen'.

Golda
(alt. Goldia, Goldie)
English, meaning 'gold'.

Grace
(alt. Graça, Gracie, Gracin, Grayce)
Latin, meaning 'grace'.

Grainne
(alt. Grania)
Irish Gaelic, meaning 'love'.

Gratia
(alt. Grasia)
Latin, meaning 'blessing'.

Greer
(alt. Grier)
Latin, meaning 'alert and watchful'.

G

Gregoria
Latin, meaning 'alert'.

Greta
(alt. Gretel)
Greek, meaning 'pearl'.

Gretchen
German, meaning 'pearl'.

Griselda
(alt. Griselle)
German, meaning 'grey fighting maid'.

Gudrun
Scandinavian, meaning 'battle'.

Guinevere
Welsh, meaning 'white and smooth'. The queen in Arthurian legend.

Gwen
Shortened form of Gwendolyn, meaning 'fair bow'.

Gwenda
Welsh, meaning 'fair and good'.

Gwendolyn
(alt. Gwendolen, Gwenel)
Welsh, meaning 'fair bow'.

Gwyneth
(alt. Gwynneth, Gwynyth)
Welsh, meaning 'happiness'.

Gwynn
(alt. Gwyn)
Welsh, meaning 'fair blessed'.

Gypsy
English, meaning 'of the Roman tribe'.

Grythao
English, meaning 'fiery'.

Names from ancient Greece

Agatha
Ariadne
Berenice
Cressida
Iliana
Lisandra
Medea
Nereida
Sophia
Xenia

G

269

English and Scottish royalty

Adelaide	Elizabeth
Alexandra	Mairi
Anna	Margaret
Anne	Mary
Catherine	Matilda
Eleanor	Victoria

G

Girls' names

Habibah
(alt. Habiba)

Arabic, meaning 'beloved'.

Hadassah
Hebrew, meaning 'myrtle tree'.

Hadley
English, meaning 'heather meadow'.

Hadria
Latin, meaning 'from Hadria'.

Hala
Arabic, meaning 'halo'.

Haley
(alt. Haelee, Haely, Hailee, Hailey, Hailie, Haleigh, Hali, Halie)

English, meaning 'hay meadow'.

Halima
(alt. Halina)

Arabic, meaning 'gentle'.

Hallie
(alt. Halle, Halley)

German, meaning 'ruler of the home or estate'.

Hannah
(alt. Haana, Hana, Hanna)

Hebrew, meaning 'grace'.

Harika

Turkish, meaning 'superior one'.

Harley
(alt. Harlene)

English, meaning 'the long field'.

Harlow

English, meaning 'army hill'.

Harmony

Latin, meaning 'harmony'.

Harper

English, meaning 'minstrel'.

Harriet
(alt. Harriett, Harriette)

German, meaning 'ruler of the home or estate'.

Hattie

Shortened form of Harriet, meaning 'ruler of the home or estate'.

Haven

English, meaning 'a place of sanctuary'.

Hayden

Old English, meaning 'hedged valley'.

Hayley
(alt. Haylee, Hayleigh, Haylie)

English, meaning 'hay meadow'.

Hazel
(alt. Hazle)

English, from the tree of the same name.

Heather

English, from the flower of the same name.

Heaven

English, meaning 'everlasting bliss'.

Hedda

German, meaning 'warfare'.

Hedwig

German, meaning 'warfare and strife'.

Heidi
(alt. Heidy)

German, meaning 'nobility'.

Helen
(alt. Halen, Helena, Helene, Hellen)
Greek, meaning 'light'.

Helga
German, meaning 'holy and sacred'.

Helia
Greek, meaning 'sun'.

Heloise
French, meaning 'renowned in war'.

Henrietta
(alt. Henriette)
German, meaning 'ruler of the house'.

Hephzibah
Hebrew, meaning 'my delight is in her'.

Hera
Greek, meaning 'queen'. The wife of Zeus in Greek mythology.

Hermia
(alt. Hermina, Hermine, Herminia)
Greek, meaning 'messenger'.

Hermione
Greek, meaning 'earthly'. Best known for the Harry Potter character.

Hero
Greek, meaning 'brave one of the people'.

Hertha
English, meaning 'earth'.

Hesper
(alt. Hesperia)
Greek, meaning 'evening star'.

Hester
(alt. Hestia)
Greek, meaning 'star'.

Hilary
(alt. Hillary)
Greek, meaning 'cheerful and happy'.

Hilda
(alt. Hildur)
German, meaning 'battle woman'.

H

Hildegarde
(alt. Hildegard)

German, meaning 'battle stronghold'.

Hildred

German, meaning 'battle counsellor'.

Hilma

German variant of Wilhelmina, meaning 'helmet'.

Hirkani

Indian, meaning 'like a diamond'.

Hollis

English, meaning 'near the holly bushes'.

Holly
(alt. Holli, Hollie)

English, from the tree of the same name.

Honey

English, from the word 'honey'.

Honor
(alt. Honour)

Latin, meaning 'woman of honour'.

Honora
(alt. Honoria)

Latin, meaning 'woman of honour'.

Hope

English, meaning 'hope'.

Hortense
(alt. Hortencia, Hortensia)

Latin, meaning 'of the garden'.

Hudson

English, meaning 'adventurous'.

Hulda

German, meaning 'loved one'.

Hyacinth

Greek, from the flower of the same name.

Girls' names

Iantha
Greek, meaning 'purple flower'.

Ichigo
Japanese, meaning 'strawberry'.

Ida
English, meaning 'prosperous'.

Idell
(alt. Idella)
English, meaning 'prosperous'.

Idona
Nordic, meaning 'renewal'.

Ignacia
Latin, meaning 'ardent'.

Ila
French, meaning 'island'.

Ilana
Hebrew, meaning 'tree'.

Ilaria
Italian, meaning 'cheerful'.

Ilene
American, meaning 'light'.

Iliana
(alt. Ileana)
Greek, meaning 'Trojan'.

Ilona
Hungarian, meaning 'light'.

Ilsa

German, meaning 'pledged to God'.

Ima

German, meaning 'embraces everything'.

Iman

Arabic, meaning 'faith'.

Imara

Hungarian, meaning 'great ruler'.

Imelda

German, meaning 'all-consuming fight'.

Imogen

(alt. Imogene)

Latin, meaning 'last-born'.

Ina

Latin, meaning 'to make feminine'.

Inaya

Arabic, meaning 'taking care'.

India

(alt. Indie)

Hindi, from the country of the same name.

Indiana

Latin, meaning 'from India'. Also a state in the US.

Indigo

Greek, meaning 'deep blue dye'.

Indira

(alt. Inira)

Sanskrit, meaning 'beauty'.

Inez

(alt. Ines)

Spanish, meaning 'pure'.

Inga

(alt. Inge, Ingeborg, Inger)

Scandinavian, meaning 'guarded by Ing'.

Ingrid

Scandinavian, meaning 'beautiful'.

Io

(alt. Eyo)

Greek, from the mythological heroine of the same name.

Ioanna

Greek, meaning 'grace'.

Iola

(alt. Iole)

Greek, meaning 'cloud of dawn'.

Iolanthe

Greek, meaning 'violet flower'.

Iona

Greek, from the island of the same name.

Ione

Greek, meaning 'violet'.

Iorwen

Welsh, meaning 'fair'.

Iphigenia

Greek, meaning 'sacrifice'.

Ira

(alt. Iva)

Hebrew, meaning 'watchful'.

Irene

(alt. Irelyn, Irena, Irina, Irini)

Greek, meaning 'peace'.

Iris

Greek, meaning 'rainbow'. Also from the flower of the same name.

Irma

German, meaning 'universal'.

Isabel

(alt. Isabela, Isabell, Isabella, Isabelle, Isabeth, Isobel, Izabella, Izabelle)

Spanish, meaning 'pledged to God'.

Isadora

Latin, meaning 'gift of Isis'.

Ishana

Hindi, meaning 'desire'.

Isis

Egyptian, from the goddess of the same name.

Isla

(alt. Isa, Isela, Isley)

Scottish Gaelic, meaning 'river'.

Isolde

Welsh, meaning 'fair lady'.

Istas

Native American, meaning 'snow'.

Ivana

Slavic, meaning 'Jehovah is gracious'.

Ivette

Variation of Yvette, meaning 'yew wood'.

Ivonne

Variation of Yvonne, meaning 'yew wood'.

Ivory

Latin, meaning 'white as elephant tusks'.

Ivy

English, from the plant of the same name.

Ixia

South African, from the flower of the same name.

Boys' names for girls (female spellings)

Alex
Billie
Cori
Charlie
Elliott
Geri
Jamie
Jo
Leslie
Riley
Robyn
Toni

J Girls' names

Jaamini

Hindi, meaning 'evening'.

Jacinda
(alt. Jacinta)
Spanish, meaning 'hyacinth'.

Jackie
(alt. Jacky, Jacque, Jacqui)
Shortened form of Jacqueline, meaning 'he who supplants'.

Jacqueline
(alt. Jacalyn, Jacklyn, Jaclyn, Jacquelin, Jacquelyn, Jacquline, Jaqlyn, Jaquelin, Jaqueline)
French, meaning 'he who supplants'.

Jade
(alt. Jada, Jaida, Jayda, Jayde)
Spanish, meaning 'green stone'.

Jaden
(alt. Jadyn, Jaiden, Jaidyn, Jayden)
Contraction of Jade and Hayden, meaning 'green hedged valley'.

Jael
Hebrew, meaning 'mountain goat'.

Jaime
(alt. Jaima, Jaimie, Jami, Jamie)
Spanish, meaning 'he who supplants'.

Jamila
Arabic, meaning 'lovely'.

279

Jan
(alt. Jann, Janna)
Hebrew, meaning 'the Lord is gracious'.

Jana
(alt. Jaana)
Hebrew, meaning 'the Lord is gracious'.

Janae
(alt. Janay)
American, meaning 'the Lord is gracious'.

Jane
(alt. Jayne)
Feminine form of the Hebrew John, meaning 'the Lord is gracious'.

Janelle
(alt. Janel, Janell, Jenelle)
American, meaning 'the Lord is gracious'.

Janet
(alt. Janette)
Scottish, meaning 'the Lord is gracious'.

Janice
(alt. Janis)
American, meaning 'the Lord is gracious'.

Janie
(alt. Janney, Jannie)
Shortened form of Janet, meaning 'the Lord is gracious'.

Janine
(alt. Janeen)
English, meaning 'the Lord is gracious'.

Janoah
(alt. Janiya, Janiyah)
Hebrew, meaning 'quiet and calm'.

January
Latin, meaning 'the first month'.

Jarita
Hindi-Sanskrit, meaning 'famous bird'.

Jasmine
(alt. Jasmin, Jazim, Jazmine)
Persian, meaning 'jasmine flower'.

Jay
Latin, meaning 'jaybird'.

Jayna
Sanskrit, meaning 'bringer of victory'.

Jean
(alt. Jeane, Jeanne)
Scottish, meaning 'the Lord is gracious'.

Jeana
(alt. Jeanna)
Latin, meaning 'queen'.

Jeanette
(alt. Jeannette, Janette)
French, meaning 'the Lord is gracious'.

Jeanie
(alt. Jeannie)
Shortened form of Jeanette, meaning 'the Lord is gracious'.

Jeanine
(alt. Jeannine)
Latin, meaning 'the Lord is gracious'.

Jemima
Hebrew, meaning 'dove'.

Jemma
English variant of Gemma, meaning 'precious stone'.

Jena
Arabic, meaning 'little bird'.

Jenna
Hebrew, meaning 'the Lord is gracious'.

Jennifer
(alt. Jenifer)
Welsh, meaning 'white and smooth'.

Flower names

Acacia
Bluebell
Daisy
Flora
Hyacinth
Lilac
Petunia
Primrose
Rose
Snowdrop

J

281

Jenny
(alt. Jennie)
Shortened form of Jennifer, meaning 'white and smooth'.

Jerrie
(alt. Jeri, Jerri, Jerrie, Jerry)
German, meaning 'spear ruler'.

Jerusha
Hebrew, meaning 'married'.

Jeryl
English, meaning 'spear ruler'.

Jessa
Shortened form of Jessica, meaning 'He sees'.

Jessamy
(alt. Jessame, Jessamine, Jessamyn)
Persian, meaning 'jasmine flower'.

Jessica
(alt. Jesica, Jesika, Jessika)
Hebrew, meaning 'He sees'.

Jessie
(alt. Jesse, Jessi, Jessye)
Shortened form of Jessica, meaning 'He sees'.

Jesusa
Spanish, meaning 'mother of the Lord'.

Jethetha
Hebrew, meaning 'princess'.

Jette
(alt. Jetta, Jettie)
Danish, meaning 'black as coal'.

Jewel
(alt. Jewell)
French, meaning 'delight'.

Jezebel
(alt. Jezabel, Jezabelle)
Hebrew, meaning 'pure and virginal'. Thought of as a term for 'bad women'.

Jill
Latin, meaning 'youthful'.

Jillian
Latin, meaning 'youthful'.

Jimena
Spanish, meaning 'heard'.

Jo

Shortened form of Joanna, meaning 'the Lord is gracious'.

Joan

Hebrew, meaning 'the Lord is gracious'.

Joanna

(alt. Joana, Joanie, Joann, Joanne, Johanna, Joni)

Hebrew, meaning 'the Lord is gracious'.

Jocasta

Italian, meaning 'lighthearted'.

Jocelyn

(alt. Jauslyn, Jocelyne, Joscelin, Joslyn)

German, meaning 'cheerful'.

Jody

(alt. Jodee, Jodi, Jodie)

Shortened form of Judith, meaning 'Jewish'.

Joelle

(alt. Joela)

Hebrew, meaning 'Jehovah is the Lord'.

Joie

French, meaning 'joy'.

Jolene

Contraction of Joanna and Darlene, meaning 'gracious darling'.

Jolie

(alt. Joely)

French, meaning 'pretty'.

Jordan

(alt. Jordana, Jordin, Jordyn)

Hebrew, meaning 'descend'.

Josephine

(alt. Josefina, Josephina)

Hebrew, meaning 'Jehovah increases'.

Josie

(alt. Joss, Jossie)

Shortened form of Josephine, meaning 'Jehovah increases'.

Jovita

(alt. Jovie)

Latin, meaning 'made glad'.

Joy

Latin, meaning 'joy'.

Joyce

Latin, meaning 'joyous'.

Juanita
(alt. Juana)
Spanish, meaning 'the Lord is gracious'.

Jubilee
Hebrew, meaning 'horn of a ram'.

Judith
(alt. Judit)
Hebrew, meaning 'Jewish'.

Judy
(alt. Judi, Judie)
Shortened form of Judith, Hebrew, meaning 'Jewish'.

Jules
French, meaning 'Jove's child'.

Julia
Latin, meaning 'youthful'.

Julianne
(alt. Juliana, Juliann, Julianne)
Latin, meaning 'youthful'

Julie
(alt. Juli)
Shortened form of Julia, meaning 'youthful'.

Juliet
(alt. Joliet, Juliette)
Latin, meaning 'youthful'. Most often associated with Shakespeare's heroine.

June
(alt. Juna)
Latin, after the month of the same name.

Juniper
Dutch, from the shrub of the same name.

Juno
(alt. Juneau)
Latin, meaning 'queen of heaven'.

Justice
English, meaning 'to deliver what is just'.

Justine
(alt. Justina)
Latin, meaning 'fair and righteous'.

Jørgina
Dutch, meaning 'farmer'.

K Girls' names

Kadenza
(alt. Kadence)
Latin, meaning 'with rhythm'.

Kadisha
Hebrew, meaning 'religious one'.

Kaitlin
(alt. Kaitlyn)
Greek, meaning 'pure'.

Kala
(alt. Kaela, Kaiala, Kaila)
Sanskrit, meaning 'black one'.

Kali
(alt. Kailee, Kailey, Kaleigh, Kaley, Kalie, Kalli, Kally, Kaylee, Kayleigh)
Sanskrit, meaning 'black one'.

Kalila
Arabic, meaning 'beloved'.

Kalina
Slavic, meaning 'flower'.

Kalliope
(alt. Calliope)
Greek, meaning 'beautiful voice'. From the muse of the same name.

Kallista
Greek, meaning 'most beautiful'.

Kama
Sanskrit, meaning 'love'.

Kami
Japanese, meaning 'lord'.

Place names

Adelaide
Atlanta
Brittany
Etna
Florence
India
Lydia
Madeira
Paris
Savannah

Kamilla
(alt. Kamilah)
Slavic, meaning 'serving girl'.

Kana
Hawaiian, from the demi-god of the same name.

Kandace
(alt. Kandice)
Latin, meaning 'glowing white'.

Kandy
(alt. Kandi)
Shortened form of Kandace, meaning 'glowing white'.

Kanika
African, meaning 'black cloth'.

Kara
Latin, meaning 'dear one'.

Karen
(alt. Karan, Karalyn, Karin, Karina, Karon, Karren)
Greek, meaning 'pure'.

Kari
(alt. Karie, Karri, Karrie)
Shortened form of Karen, meaning 'pure'.

Karimah
Arabic, meaning 'giving'.

Karishma
Sanskrit, meaning 'miracle'.

Karla
German, meaning 'man'.

Karly
(alt. Karlee, Karley, Karli)
German, meaning 'free man'.

Karlyn
German, meaning 'man'.

Karma
Hindi, meaning 'destiny'.

K

Karol
(alt. Karolina, Karolyn)
Slavic, meaning 'little and womanly'.

Kasey
(alt. Kacey, Kaci, Kacie, Kacy, Kasie, Kassie)
Irish Gaelic, meaning 'alert and watchful'.

Kassandra
Greek, meaning 'she who entangles men'.

Kasumi
Japanese, meaning 'of the mist'.

Katarina
(alt. Katarine, Katerina, Katharina)
Greek, meaning 'pure'.

Kate
(alt. Kat, Katie, Kathi, Kathie, Kathy, Kati, Katy)
Shortened form of Katherine, meaning 'pure'.

Katelyn
(alt. Katelin, Katelynn, Katlin, Katlyn)
Greek, meaning 'pure'.

Katherine
(alt. Katharine, Katheryn, Kathrine, Kathryn)
Greek, meaning 'pure'.

Kathleen
(alt. Kathlyn)
Greek, meaning 'pure'.

Katrina
(alt. Katina)
Greek, meaning 'pure'.

Kaveri
Indian, meaning 'sacred river'.

Kay
(alt. Kaye)
Shortened form of Katherine, meaning 'pure'.

Kaya
Sanskrit, meaning 'nature', or Turkish, meaning 'rock'.

Kayla
(alt. Kaylah)
Greek, meaning 'pure'.

Kayley
(alt. Kayley, Kayli)
American, meaning 'pure'.

Kaylin
American, meaning 'pure'.

Keeley
(alt. Keely)
Irish, meaning 'battle maid'.

Keila
Hebrew, meaning 'citadel'.

Keira
Irish Gaelic, meaning 'dark'.

Keisha
(alt. Keesha)
Arabic, meaning 'woman'.

Kelis
American, meaning 'beautiful'.

Kelly
(alt. Keli, Kelley, Kelli, Kellie)
Irish Gaelic, meaning 'battle maid'.

Kelsey
(alt. Kelcee, Kelcie, Kelsea, Kelsi, Kelsie)
English, meaning 'island'.

Kendall
(alt. Kendal)
English, meaning 'the valley of the River Kent'. Also a place in Cumbria.

Kendra
English, meaning 'knowing'.

Kenna
Irish Gaelic, meaning 'handsome'.

Kennedy
(alt. Kenadee, Kennedi)
Irish Gaelic, meaning 'helmet head'.

Kenzie
Shortened form of McKenzie, meaning 'son of the wise ruler'.

Kerensa
Cornish, meaning 'love'.

Kerrigan
Irish, meaning 'black haired'.

Kerry
(alt. Keri, Kerri, Kerrie)
Irish, from the county of the same name.

Khadijah
(alt. Khadejah)
Arabic, meaning 'premature baby'.

Kiana
(alt. Kia, Kiana)
American, meaning 'fibre'.

Kiara
Italian, meaning 'light'.

Kiki
Spanish, meaning 'home ruler'.

Kim
Shortened form of Kimberly, from the town of the same name.

Kimana
Native American, meaning 'butterfly'.

Kimberly
(alt. Kimberleigh, Kimberley)
Old English, meaning 'royal forest'.

Kingsley
(alt. Kinsley)
English, meaning 'king's meadow'.

Kinsey
English, meaning 'king's victory'.

Kira
Greek, meaning 'lady'.

Kiri
Maori, meaning 'tree bark'.

Long names
Alexandra
Benedicta
Christabelle
Constantine
Emmanuelle
Gabrielle
Henrietta
Philomena
Rosamond
Virginia

Kirsten
(alt. Kirstin)
Scandinavian, meaning 'Christian'.

Kirstie
(alt. Kirsty)
Shortened form of Kirsten, meaning 'Christian'.

Kitty
(alt. Kittie)
Shortened form of Katherine, meaning 'pure'.

Kizzy
Hebrew, meaning the plant 'cassia'.

Klara

Hungarian, meaning 'bright'.

Komal

Hindi, meaning 'soft and tender'.

Konstantina

Latin, meaning 'steadfast'.

Kora
(alt. Kori)

Greek, meaning 'maiden'.

Kris
(alt. Krista, Kristi, Kristie, Kristy)

Shortened form of Kristen, meaning 'Christian'.

Kristen
(alt. Kristan, Kristin, Kristine, Krysten)

Greek, meaning 'Christian'.

Krystal
(alt. Kristal, Kristel)

Greek, meaning 'ice'.

Kwanza
(alt. Kwanzaa)

African, meaning 'beginning'.

Kyla
(alt. Kya, Kylah, Kyle)

Scottish, meaning 'narrow spit of land'.

Kylie
(alt. Kiley, Kylee)

Irish Gaelic, meaning 'graceful'.

Kyoko

Japanese, meaning 'girl who sees her own true image'.

Kyra

Greek, meaning 'lady'.

Kyrie

Greek, meaning 'the Lord'.

Short names

Ali
Bev
Fay
Jan
Jo
Kay
Lyn
May
Nia
Val

L Girls' names

Lacey
(alt. Laci, Lacie, Lacy)
French, from a nobleman's surname.

Ladonna
Italian, meaning 'lady'.

Lady
English, meaning 'bread kneader'.

Laidh
Hebrew, meaning 'lioness'.

Laila
(alt. Laelia, Layla, Leila, Lejla, Lela, Lelah, Lelia)
Arabic, meaning 'night'.

Lainey
(alt. Laine, Laney)
French, meaning 'bright light'.

Lakeisha
(alt. Lakeshia)
American, meaning 'woman'.

Lakshmi
(alt. Laxmi)
Sanskrit, meaning 'good omen'. Also the Hindu goddess.

Lana
Greek, meaning 'light'.

Lani
(alt. Lanie)
Hawaiian, meaning 'sky'.

Lara
Latin, meaning 'famous'.

291

Laraine
French, meaning 'from Lorraine'.

Larissa
(alt. Larisa)
Greek, meaning 'lighthearted'.

Lark
(alt. Larkin)
English, meaning 'playful songbird'.

Larsen
Scandinavian, meaning 'son of Lars'.

Latifa
Arabic, meaning 'gentle and pleasant'.

Latika
(alt. Lotika)
Hindi, meaning 'a plant'.

Latisha
Latin, meaning 'happiness'.

Latona
(alt. Latonia)
Roman, from the mythological heroine of the same name.

Latoya
Spanish, meaning 'victorious one'.

Latrice
(alt. Latricia)
Latin, meaning 'noble'.

Laura
(alt. Lora)
Latin, meaning 'laurel'.

Laurel
Latin, meaning 'laurel tree'.

Lauren
(alt. Lauran, Loren)
Latin, meaning 'laurel'.

Laveda
(alt. Lavada)
Latin, meaning 'cleansed'.

Lavender
Latin, from the plant of the same name.

Laverne
(alt. Lavern, Laverna)
Latin, from the goddess of the same name.

L

Lavinia
(alt. Lavina)

Latin, meaning 'woman of Rome'.

Lavita

American, meaning 'charming'.

Lavonne
(alt. Lavon)

French, meaning 'yew wood'.

Leah
(alt. Lea, Leia)

Hebrew, meaning 'weary'.

Leandra

Greek, meaning 'lion man'.

Leanne
(alt. Leann, Leanna, Leeann)

Contraction of Lee and Ann, meaning 'meadow grace'.

Leda

Greek, meaning 'gladness'.

Lee
(alt. Leigh)

English, meaning 'pasture or meadow'.

'Bad girl' names

Desdemona
Diva
Fifi
Lilith
Pandora
Peaches
Sadie
Scarlett
Tallulah
Xena

Leilani

Hawaiian, meaning 'flower from heaven'.

Leith

Scottish Gaelic, meaning 'broad river'.

Lena
(alt. Leena, Lina)

Latin, meaning 'light'.

Lenna
(alt. Lennie)

German, meaning 'lion's strength'.

Lenore
(alt. Lenora)

Greek, meaning 'light'.

L

Léonie
(alt. Leona, Leone)
Latin, meaning 'lion'.

Leonora
(alt. Leonor, Leonore)
Greek, meaning 'light'.

Leora
Greek, meaning 'light'.

Lerola
Latin, meaning 'like a blackbird'.

Leslie
(alt. Leslee, Lesley, Lesli)
Scottish Gaelic, meaning 'the grey castle'.

Leta
Latin, meaning 'glad and joyful'.

Letha
Greek, meaning 'forgetfulness'.

Letitia
(alt. Leticia, Lettice, Lettie)
Latin, meaning 'joy and gladness'.

Lexia
(alt. Lexi, Lexie)
Greek, meaning 'defender of mankind'.

Lia
Italian, meaning 'bringer of the gospel'.

Liana
French, meaning 'to twine around'.

Libby
(alt. Libbie)
Shortened form of Elizabeth, meaning 'consecrated to God'.

Liberty
English, meaning 'freedom'.

Lida
Slavic, meaning 'loved by the people'.

Liese
(alt. Liesel, Liesl)
German, meaning 'pledged to God'.

Lila
(alt. Lilah)
Arabic, meaning 'night'.

Lilac

Latin, from the flower of the same name.

Lilia

(alt. Lilias)

Scottish, meaning 'lily'.

Lilith

Arabic, meaning 'ghost'.

Lillian

(alt. Lilian, Liliana, Lilla, Lillianna)

Latin, meaning 'lily'.

Lily

(alt. Lili, Lillie, Lilly)

Latin, from the flower of the same name.

Linda

(alt. Lynda)

Spanish, meaning 'pretty'.

Linden

(alt. Lindie, Lindy)

European, from the tree of the same name.

Lindsay

(alt. Lindsey, Linsey)

English, meaning 'island of linden trees'.

Linette

Welsh, meaning 'idol'.

Linnea

(alt. Linnae, Linny)

Scandinavian, meaning 'lime or linden tree'.

Liora

(alt. Lior)

Hebrew, meaning 'I have a light'.

Lirit

Hebrew, meaning 'musically talented'.

Lisa

(alt. Leesa, Lise, Liza)

Hebrew, meaning 'pledged to God'.

Lissa

Greek, meaning 'bee'.

Lissandra

(alt. Lisandra)

Greek, meaning 'man's defender'.

Liv

Nordic, meaning 'defence'.

Famous female singers

Adele (Adkins)
Annie (Lennox)
Billie (Holiday)
Dinah (Washington)
Ella (Fitzgerald)
Etta (James)
Florence (Welch)
Judy (Garland)
Kate (Bush)
Kylie (Minogue)
Lily (Allen)
Nina (Simone)

Livia
Latin, meaning 'olive'.

Liz
(alt. Lizzie, Lizzy)
Shortened form of Elizabeth, meaning 'consecrated to God'.

Logan
Irish Gaelic, meaning 'small hollow'.

Lois
German, meaning 'renowned in battle'.

Lola
Spanish, meaning 'sorrows'.

Lolita
(alt. Lollie)
Spanish, meaning 'sorrows'.

Lona
Latin, meaning 'lion'.

Lora
Latin, meaning 'laurel'.

Lorelei
(alt. Loralai, Loralie)
German, meaning 'dangerous rock'.

Lorenza
Latin, meaning 'from Laurentium'.

Loretta
(alt. Loreto)
Latin, meaning 'laurel'.

Lori
(alt. Laurie, Lorie, Lorri)
Latin, meaning 'laurel'.

Lorna
Scottish, from the town of Lorne.

L

Lorraine
(alt. *Loraine*)
French, meaning 'from Lorraine'.

Lottie
(alt. *Lotta, Lotte*)
French, meaning 'little and womanly'.

Lotus
Greek, meaning 'lotus flower'.

Lou
(alt. *Louie, Lue*)
Shortened form of Louise, meaning 'renowned in battle'.

Louise
(alt. *Louisa, Luisa*)
German, meaning 'renowned in battle'.

Lourdes
French, from the town of the same name.

Love
English, from the word 'love'.

Lowri
Welsh, meaning 'crowned with laurels'.

Luanne
(alt. *Luann, Luanna*)
German, meaning 'renowned in battle'.

Luba
Hebrew, meaning 'dearly loved'.

Lucia
(alt. *Luciana*)
Italian, meaning 'light'.

Lucille
(alt. *Lucile, Lucilla*)
French, meaning 'light'.

Lucinda
English, meaning 'light'.

Lucretia
(alt. *Lucrece*)
Spanish, meaning 'light'.

Lucy
(alt. *Lucie*)
Latin, meaning 'light'.

Ludmilla
Slavic, meaning 'beloved of the people'.

L

Luella
(alt. Lue)

English, meaning 'renowned in battle'.

Lulu
(alt. Lula)

German, meaning 'renowned in battle'.

Luna

Latin, meaning 'moon'.

Lupita

Spanish, short form of Guadelupe. From the town of the same name.

Luz

Spanish, meaning 'light'.

Lydia
(alt. Lidia)

Greek, meaning 'from Lydia'.

Lynn
(alt. Lyn, Lynne)

Spanish, meaning 'pretty';
English, meaning 'waterfall'.

Lynton

English, meaning 'town of lime trees'.

Lyra

Latin, meaning 'lyre'.

Tennis players

Anna (Kournikova)
Billie Jean (King)
Heather (Watson)
Justine (Henin)
Laura (Robson)
Maria (Sharapova)
Monica (Seles)
Serena (Williams)
Sue (Barker)
Steffi (Graf)
Venus (Williams)

L

 Girls' names

Mab
Irish Gaelic, meaning 'joy'.

Mabel
(alt. Mabelle, Mable)
Latin, meaning 'loveable'.

Macaria
Spanish, meaning 'blessed'.

Machiko
Japanese, meaning 'beautiful woman'.

Macy
(alt. Macey, Maci, Macie)
French, meaning 'Matthew's estate'.

Mada
English, meaning 'from Magdala'.

Madaio
Hawaiian, meaning 'gift from God'.

Madden
(alt. Maddyn)
Irish, meaning 'little dog'.

Maddie
(alt. Maddi, Maddie, Madie)
Shortened form of Madeline, meaning 'from Magdala'.

Madeline
(alt. Madaline, Madalyn, Madeleine, Madelyn, Madelynn, Madilyn)
Greek, meaning 'from Magdala'.

Madge
Greek, meaning 'pearl'.

Madhuri

Hindi, meaning 'sweet girl'.

Madison

(alt. Maddison, Madisen, Madisyn, Madyson)

English, meaning 'son of the mighty warrior'.

Madonna

Latin, meaning 'my lady'.

Maeve

Irish Gaelic, meaning 'intoxicating'.

Mafalda

Spanish, meaning 'battle-mighty'.

Magali

Greek, meaning 'pearl'.

Magdalene

(alt. Magdalen, Magdalena)

Greek, meaning 'from Magdala'.

Maggie

Shortened form of Margaret, meaning 'pearl'.

Magnolia

Latin, from the flower of the same name.

Mahala

(alt. Mahalia)

Hebrew, meaning 'tender affection'.

Maia

(alt. Maja)

Greek, meaning 'mother'.

Maida

English, meaning 'maiden'.

Maisie

(alt. Maisey, Maisy, Maizie, Masie, Mazie)

Greek, meaning 'pearl'.

Malin

Hebrew and English, meaning 'of Magdala'.

Maliyah

Hawaiian, meaning 'beloved'.

Malka

Hebrew, meaning 'queen'.

Mallory
(alt. Malorie)
French, meaning 'unhappy'.

Malvina
Gaelic, meaning 'smooth brow'.

Mamie
(alt. Mammie)
Shortened form of Margaret, meaning 'pearl'.

Mandy
(alt. Mandie)
Shortened form of Amanda, meaning 'much loved'.

Manisha
Sanskrit, meaning 'desire'.

Mansi
Hopi, meaning 'plucked flower'.

Manuela
Spanish, meaning 'the Lord is among us'.

Mara
Hebrew, meaning 'bitter'.

Marcela
(alt. Marceline, Marcella, Marcelle)
Latin, meaning 'war-like'.

Marcia
Latin, meaning 'war-like'.

Marcy
(alt. Marci, Marcie)
Latin, meaning 'war-like'.

Margaret
(alt. Margarete, Margaretta, Margarette, Margret)
Greek, meaning 'pearl'.

Margery
(alt. Marge, Margie, Margit, Margy)
French, meaning 'pearl'.

Margo
(alt. Margot)
French, meaning 'pearl'.

Marguerite
(alt. Margarita)
French, meaning 'pearl'.

Maria
(alt. Mariah)
Latin, meaning 'bitter'.

Marian
(alt. Mariam, Mariana, Marion)
French, meaning 'bitter grace'.

Marianne
(alt. Mariana, Mariann,
Maryann, Maryanne)
French, meaning 'bitter grace'.

Maribel
American, meaning 'bitterly
beautiful'.

Marie
French, meaning 'bitter'.

Mariel
(alt. Mariela, Mariella)
Dutch, meaning 'bitter'.

Marietta
(alt. Marieta)
French, meaning 'bitter'.

Marigold
English, from the flower of the
same name.

Marika
Dutch, meaning 'bitter'.

Marilyn
(alt. Marilee, Marilene,
Marilynn)
English, meaning 'bitter'.

Marina
(alt. Marine)
Latin, meaning 'from the sea'.

Mariposa
Spanish, meaning 'butterfly'.

Marisa
(alt. Maris)
Latin, meaning 'of the sea'.

Marisol
Spanish, meaning 'bitter sun'.

Marissa
American, meaning 'of the sea'.

Marjolaine
French, meaning 'marjoram'.

Marjorie
(alt. Marjory)
French, meaning 'pearl'.

Marla
Shortened form of Marlene,
meaning 'bitter'.

Marlene
(alt. Marlen, Marlena)
Hebrew, meaning 'bitter'.

Marley
(alt. Marlee)
American, meaning 'bitter'.

Marlo
(alt. Marlowe)
American, meaning 'bitter'.

Marnie
(alt. Marney)
Scottish, meaning 'from the sea'.

Marseille
French, from the city of the same name.

Marsha
English, meaning 'war-like'.

Martha
(alt. Marta)
Aramaic, meaning 'lady'.

Martina
Latin, meaning 'war-like'.

Marvel
French, meaning 'something to marvel at'.

Mary
Hebrew, meaning 'bitter'.

Masada
Hebrew, meaning 'foundation'.

Matilda
(alt. Mathilda, Mathilde, Matide)
German, meaning 'battle-mighty'.

Mattea
Hebrew, meaning 'gift of God'.

Maude
(alt. Maud)
German, meaning 'battle-mighty'.

Maura
Irish, meaning 'bitter'.

Maureen
(alt. Maurine)
Irish, meaning 'bitter'.

Mavis
French, meaning 'thrush'.

Maxine
(alt. Maxie)
Latin, meaning 'greatest'.

M

May
(alt. Mae, Maya, Maye, Mayra)
Hebrew, meaning 'gift of God'.
Also the month.

Mckenna
(alt. Mackenna)
Irish Gaelic, meaning 'son of the handsome one'.

Mckenzie
(alt. Mackenzie, Mckenzy, Mikenzi)
Irish Gaelic, meaning 'son of the wise ruler'.

Meara
Gaelic, meaning 'filled with happiness'.

Medea
(alt. Meda)
Greek, meaning 'ruling'.

Meg
Shortened form of Margaret, meaning 'pearl'.

Megan
(alt. Meagan, Meghan)
Welsh, meaning 'pearl'.

Mehri
Persian, meaning 'kind'.

Meiwei
Chinese, meaning 'forever enchanting'.

Melanie
(alt. Melania, Melany, Melonie)
Greek, meaning 'dark-skinned'.

Melba
Australian, meaning 'from Melbourne'.

Melia
(alt. Meliah)
German, meaning 'industrious'.

Melina
Greek, meaning 'honey'.

Melinda
Latin, meaning 'honey'.

Melisande
French, meaning 'bee'.

Melissa
(alt. Melisa, Mellissa)
Greek, meaning 'bee'.

Melody
(alt. Melodie)
Greek, meaning 'song'.

Melvina
Celtic, meaning 'chieftain'.

Menora
Hebrew, meaning 'candlestick'.

Mercedes
Spanish, meaning 'mercies'.
Most often associated with
the car.

Mercy
English, meaning 'mercy'.

Meredith
(alt. Meridith)
Welsh, meaning 'great ruler'.

Merle
French, meaning 'blackbird'.

Merry
English, meaning 'lighthearted'.

Meryl
(alt. Merrill)
Irish Gaelic, meaning 'sea-
bright'.

Meta
German, meaning 'pearl'.

Mia
Italian, meaning 'mine'.

Michaela
*(alt. Makaela, Makaila, Micaela,
Mikaila, Mikayla)*
Hebrew, meaning 'who is like
the Lord'.

Michelle
*(alt. Machelle, Mechelle,
Michaele, Michal, Michele)*
French, meaning 'who is like
the Lord'.

Mickey
(alt. Micki, Mickie)
Shortened form of Michelle,
meaning 'who is like the Lord'.

Mieko
Japanese, meaning 'born into
wealth'.

Migdalia
Greek, meaning 'from
Magdala'.

Mignon
French, meaning 'cute'.

M

Mika
(alt. Micah)
Hebrew, meaning 'who
resembles God'.

Milada
Czech, meaning 'my love'.

Milagros
Spanish, meaning 'miracles'.

Milan
Italian, from the city of the
same name.

Mildred
English, meaning 'gentle
strength'.

Milena
Czech, meaning 'love and
warmth'.

Miley
American, meaning 'smiley'.
Made popular by Miley Cyrus.

Millicent
German, meaning 'high-born
power'.

Millie
(alt. Milly)
Shortened form of Millicent,
meaning 'high-born power'.

Mimi
Italian, meaning 'bitter'.

Popular song names

Alice ('All the Girls Love Alice', Elton John)
Billie Jean ('Billie Jean', Michael Jackson)
Caroline ('Sweet Caroline', Neil Diamond)
Delilah ('Delilah', Tom Jones)
Eileen ('Come on Eileen', Dexy's Midnight Runners)
Eleanor ('Eleanor Rigby', The Beatles)
Roxanne ('Roxanne', The Police)
Ruby ('Ruby', Kaiser Chiefs)
Sally ('Mustang Sally', Wilson Pickett)
Valerie ('Valerie', Amy Winehouse and Mark Ronson)

Mina
(alt. Mena)
German, meaning 'love'.

Mindy
(alt. Mindi)
Latin, meaning 'honey'.

Minerva
Roman, from the goddess of the same name.

Ming
Chinese, meaning 'bright'.

Minna
German, meaning 'helmet'.

Minnie
German, meaning 'helmet'. Often associated with the Disney character Minnie Mouse.

Mira
Latin, meaning 'admirable'.

Mirabel
(alt. Mirabella, Mirabelle)
Latin, meaning 'wonderful'.

Miranda
(alt. Meranda)
Latin, meaning 'admirable'.

Mirella
(alt. Mireille, Mirela)
Latin, meaning 'admirable'.

Miriam
Hebrew, meaning 'bitter'.

Mirta
Spanish, meaning 'crown of thorns'.

Missy
Shortened form of Melissa, meaning 'bee'.

Misty
(alt. Misti)
English, meaning 'mist'.

Mitzi
German, meaning 'bitter'.

Miu
Japanese, meaning 'beautiful feather'.

Moira
(alt. Maira)
Irish, meaning 'bitter'.

M

Molly
(alt. Mollie)
American, meaning 'bitter'.

Mona
Irish Gaelic, meaning 'aristocratic'.

Monica
(alt. Monika, Monique)
Latin, meaning 'adviser'.

Monroe
Gaelic, meaning 'mouth of the river Rotha'.

Montserrat
(alt. Monserrate)
Spanish, from the town of the same name.

Morag
Scottish, meaning 'star of the sea'.

Morgan
(alt. Morgann)
Welsh, meaning 'great and bright'.

Moriah
Hebrew, meaning 'the Lord is my teacher'.

Morwenna
Welsh, meaning 'maiden'.

Moselle
(alt. Mozell, Mozella, Mozelle)
Hebrew, meaning 'saviour'.

Mulan
Chinese, meaning 'wood orchid'.

Munin
Scandinavian, meaning 'good memory'.

Muriel
Irish Gaelic, meaning 'sea-bright'.

Mya
(alt. Myah)
Greek, meaning 'mother'.

Myfanwy
Welsh, meaning 'my little lovely one'.

Myra
Latin, meaning 'scented oil'.

Myrna
(alt. Mirna)
Irish Gaelic, meaning 'tender and beloved'.

Myrtle
Irish, from the shrub of the same name.

M

 Girls' names

Nadia
(alt. Nadya)
Russian, meaning 'hope'.

Nadine
French, meaning 'hope'.

Nahara
Aramaic, meaning 'light'.

Naima
Arabic, meaning 'water nymph'.

Nakia
Egyptian, meaning 'pure'.

Nalani
Hawaiian, meaning 'serenity of the skies'.

Nan
(alt. Nanna, Nannie)
Hebrew, meaning 'grace'.

Nancy
(alt. Nanci, Nancie)
Hebrew, meaning 'grace'.

Nanette
(alt. Nannette)
French, meaning 'grace'.

Naomi
(alt. Naoma, Noemi)
Hebrew, meaning 'pleasant'.

Narcissa
Greek, meaning 'daffodil'.

Nastasia

Greek, meaning 'resurrection'.

Natalie

(alt. Natalee, Natalia, Natalya, Nathalie)

Latin, meaning 'birth day'.

Natasha

(alt. Natasa)

Russian, meaning 'birth day'.

Natividad

Spanish, meaning 'Christmas'.

Neda

English, meaning 'wealthy'.

Nedra

English, meaning 'underground'.

Neema

Swahili, meaning 'born of prosperity'.

Neka

Native American, meaning 'goose'.

Nell

(alt. Nelda, Nell, Nella, Nellie, Nelly)

Shortened form of Eleanor, meaning 'light'.

Nemi

Italian, from the lake of the same name.

Neoma

Greek, meaning 'new moon'.

Nereida

Spanish, meaning 'sea nymph'.

Nerissa

Greek, meaning 'sea nymph'.

Nettie

(alt. Neta)

Shortened form of Henrietta, meaning 'ruler of the house'.

Neva

Spanish, meaning 'snowy'.

Nevaeh

American, meaning 'heaven'.

Nhung

Vietnamese, meaning 'velvet'.

Niamh
(alt. Neve)
Irish, meaning 'brightness'.

Nicki
(alt. Nicky, Nikki)
Shortened form of Nicola, meaning 'victory of the people'.

Nicola
Greek, meaning 'victory of the people'.

Nicole
(alt. Nichol, Nichole, Nicolette, Nicolle, Nikolc)
Greek, meaning 'victory of the people'.

Nidia
Spanish, meaning 'graceful'.

Nigella
Irish Gaelic, meaning 'champion'.

Nikita
Greek, meaning 'unconquered'.

Nila
Egyptian, meaning 'Nile'.

Nilda
German, meaning 'battle woman'.

Nimra
Arabic, meaning 'number'.

Nina
Spanish, meaning 'girl'.

Nissa
Hebrew, meaning 'sign'.

Nita
Spanish, meaning 'gracious'.

Nixie
German, meaning 'water sprite'.

Noel
(alt. Noelle)
French, meaning 'Christmas'.

Nola
Irish Gaelic, meaning 'white shoulder'.

Nona
Latin, meaning 'ninth'.

Nora
(alt. Norah)

Shortened form of Eleanor, meaning 'light'.

Noreen
(alt. Norine)

Irish, meaning 'light'.

Norma

Latin, meaning 'pattern'.

Normandie
(alt. Normandy)

French, from the province of the same name.

Novia

Latin, meaning 'new'.

Nuala

Irish Gaelic, meaning 'white shoulder'.

Nydia

Latin, meaning 'nest'.

Nyimbo

Swahili, meaning 'song'.

Nysa
(alt. Nyssa)

Greek, meaning 'ambition'.

Names of goddesses

Aphrodite (Love: Greek)
Ceres (Agriculture: Roman)
Eos (Dawn: Greek)
Hestia (Hearth: Greek)
Kali (Death: Hindu)
Lucinda (Childbirth: Roman)
Minerva (Wisdom: Roman)
Nephthys (Death: Egyptian)
Sesheta (Stars: Egyptian)
Terra (Earth: Roman)

N

 Girls' names

Oceana
(alt. Ocean, Océane, Ocie)
Greek, meaning 'ocean'.

Octavia
Latin, meaning 'eighth'.

Oda
(alt. Odie)
Shortened form of Odessa,
meaning 'long voyage'.

Odele
(alt. Odell)
English, meaning 'woad hill'.

Odelia
Hebrew, meaning 'I will praise
the Lord'.

Odessa
Greek, meaning 'long voyage'.

Odette
(alt. Odetta)
French, meaning 'wealthy'.

Odile
(alt. Odilia)
French, meaning 'prospers in
battle'.

Odina
Feminine form of Odin, from
the Nordic god of the same
name, meaning 'creative
inspiration'.

Odyssey
Greek, meaning 'long journey'.

Oksana
Russian, meaning 'praise to God'.

Ola
(alt. Olie)
Greek, meaning 'man's defender'.

Olena
(alt. Olene)
Russian, meaning 'light'.

Olga
Russian, meaning 'holy'.

Oliana
American, meaning 'the Lord has answered'.

Olivia
(alt. Olivev, Oliviana, Olivié)
Latin, meaning 'olive'. The UK's most popular girls' name in 2011.

Ollie
Shortened form of Olivia, meaning 'olive'.

Olwen
Welsh, meaning 'white footprint'.

Olympia
(alt. Olimpia)
Greek, meaning 'from Mount Olympus'.

Oma
(alt. Omie)
Arabic, meaning 'leader'.

Omyra
Latin, meaning 'scented oil'.

Ona
(alt. Onnie)
Shortened form of Oneida, meaning 'long awaited'.

Ondine
French, meaning 'wave of water'.

Oneida
Native American, meaning 'long awaited'.

Onyx
Latin, meaning 'veined gem'.

Oona
Irish, meaning 'unity'.

Opal
Sanskrit, meaning 'gem'.

Ophelia
(alt. Ofelia, Ophélie)
Greek, meaning 'help'. Best known from Shakespeare's play *Hamlet*.

Oprah
Hebrew, meaning 'young deer'. Most often associated with Oprah Winfrey.

Ora
Latin, meaning 'prayer'.

Orabela
Latin, meaning 'prayer'.

Colour names

Azure
Cinnabar
Ebony
Fuchsia
Ivory
Olive
Rose
Saffron
Sienna
Violet

Oralie
(alt. Oralia)
French, meaning 'golden'.

Orane
French, meaning 'rising'.

Orchid
Greek, from the flower of the same name.

Oriana
(alt. Oriane)
Latin, meaning 'dawning'.

Orla
(alt. Orlaith, Orly)
Irish Gaelic, meaning 'golden lady'.

Orlean
French, meaning 'plum'.

Ornelia
Italian, meaning 'flowering ash tree'.

Orsa
(alt. Osia, Ossie)
Latin, meaning 'bear'.

Otthid

Greek, meaning 'prospers in battle'.

Ottilie
(alt. Ottie)

French, meaning 'prospers in battle'.

Ouida

French, meaning 'renowned in battle'.

Oyintsa

Native American, meaning 'white duck'.

Ozette

Native American, from the village of the same name.

Popular North American names

Abigail	Isabella
Ava	Madison
Chloe	Mia
Emily	Olivia
Emma	Sophia

O

Girls' names

Pacifica
(alt. Pacifika)

Spanish, meaning 'peaceful'.

Padma

Sanskrit, meaning 'lotus'.

Paige
(alt. Page)

French, meaning 'serving boy'.

Paisley

Scottish, from the town of the same name.

Palma
(alt. Palmira)

Latin, meaning 'palm tree'.

Paloma

Spanish, meaning 'dove'.

Pam

Shortened form of Pamela, meaning 'all honey'.

Pamela
(alt. Pamala, Pamella, Pamla)

Greek, meaning 'all honey'.

Pandora

Greek, meaning 'all gifted'. Also from the Greek myth.

Pangiota

Greek, meaning 'all is holy'.

Paniz

Persian, meaning 'candy'.

Pansy

French, from the flower of the same name.

Paprika
English, meaning 'spice'.

Paradisa
(alt. Paradis)
Greek, meaning 'garden orchard'.

Paris
(alt. Parisa)
Greek, from the mythological hero of the same name. Also from the city.

Parker
English, meaning 'park keeper'.

Parthenia
Greek, meaning 'virginal'.

Parthenope
Greek, from the mythological Siren of the same name.

Parvati
Sanskrit, meaning 'daughter of the mountain'.

Pascale
French, meaning 'Easter'.

Pat
(alt. Patsy, Patti, Pattie, Patty)
Shortened form of Patricia, meaning 'noble'.

Patience
French, meaning 'the state of being patient'.

Patricia
(alt. Patrice)
Latin, meaning 'noble'.

Paula
Latin, meaning 'small'.

Pauline
(alt. Paulette, Paulina)
Latin, meaning 'small'.

Paxton
Latin, meaning 'peaceful town'.

Paz
Spanish, meaning 'peace'.

Pazia
Hebrew, meaning 'golden'.

Peace
English, meaning 'peace'.

P

Gem and precious stone names

Amber
Beryl
Coral
Esmeralda
Jade
Marjorie
Pearl
Ruby
Topaz

Peaches
English, meaning 'peaches'.

Pearl
(alt. Pearle, Pearlie, Perla)
Latin, meaning 'pale gemstone'.

Peggy
(alt. Peggie)
Greek, meaning 'pearl'.

Pelia
Hebrew, meaning 'marvel of God'.

Penelope
Greek, meaning 'bobbin worker'.

Penny
(alt. Penni, Pennie)
Greek, meaning 'bobbin worker'.

Peony
Greek, from the flower of the same name.

Perdita
Latin, meaning 'lost'.

Peri
(alt. Perri)
Hebrew, meaning 'outcome'.

Perry
French, meaning 'pear tree'.

Persephone
Greek, meaning 'bringer of destruction'.

Petra
(alt. Petrina)
Greek, meaning 'rock'.

Petula
Latin, meaning 'to seek'.

P

Petunia

Greek, from the flower of the same name.

Phaedra

Greek, meaning 'bright'.

Philippa

Greek, meaning 'horse lover'.

Philomena
(alt. Philoma)

Greek, meaning 'loved one'.

Phoebe

Greek, meaning 'shining and brilliant'.

Phoenix

Greek, meaning 'red as blood'. Also from the mythical bird.

Phyllida

Greek, meaning 'leafy bough'.

Phyllis
(alt. Phillia, Phylis)

Greek, meaning 'leafy bough'.

Pia

Latin, meaning 'pious'.

Piera

Italian, meaning 'rock'.

Pilar

Spanish, meaning 'pillar'.

Piper

English, meaning 'pipe player'.

Pippa

Shortened form of Philippa, meaning 'horse lover'.

Popular Asian names

Amaya	Kai
Aoi	Miya
Hana	Murasaki
Hiro	Niu
Iku	Rei

P

Plum

Latin, from the fruit of the same name.

Polly

Hebrew, meaning 'bitter'.

Pomona

Latin, meaning 'apple'.

Poppy

Latin, from the flower of the same name.

Portia
(alt. Porsha)

Latin, meaning 'from the Portia clan'.

Posy

English, meaning 'small flower'.

Precious

Latin, meaning 'of great worth'.

Priela

Hebrew, meaning 'fruit of God'.

Primavera

Italian, meaning 'springtime'.

Primrose

English, meaning 'first rose'.

Princess

English, meaning 'daughter of the monarch'.

Priscilla
(alt. Prisca, Priscila)

Latin, meaning 'ancient'.

Priya

Hindi, meaning 'loved one'.

Prudence

Latin, meaning 'caution'.

Prudie

Shortened form of Prudence, meaning 'caution'.

Prunella

Latin, meaning 'small plum'.

Psyche

Greek, meaning 'breath'. Also from Greek mythology and psychological theory.

P

Names with positive meanings

Allegra – cheerful
Augusta – magnificent
Felicia – lucky
Gladys – glad
Hilary – cheerful

Lucy – light
Phoebe – radiant
Rinah – joyful
Thalia – flourishing
Yoko – positive

Q Girls' names

Qiana
(alt. Qianah, Qiania, Qyana, Qianne)
American, meaning 'gracious'.

Qiturah
Arabic, meaning 'incense'.

Queen
(alt. Queenie)
English, meaning 'queen'.

Quiana
American, meaning 'silky'.

Quincy
(alt. Quincey)
French, meaning 'estate of the fifth son'.

Quinn
Irish Gaelic, meaning 'counsel'.

Quintessa
Latin, meaning 'creative'.

Palindrome names

Aja	Ette
Anna	Eve
Anona	Hannah
Elle	Ono
Emme	Viv

Foreign alternatives

Emily – Emilie, Emeline
Helen – Galina, Helene
Julia – Giulia, Jalia
Mary – Marie, Maria, Marjan
Sarah – Sara, Sarine, Zara
Violet – Iolanthe, Yolanda

 Girls' names

Rachel
(alt. Rachael, Rachelle)
Hebrew, meaning 'ewe'.

Radhika
Sanskrit, meaning 'prosperous'.

Rae
(alt. Ray)
Shortened form of Rachel, meaning 'ewe'.

Rafferty
Irish, meaning 'abundance'.

Rahima
Arabic, meaning 'compassionate'.

Raina
(alt. Rain, Raine, Rainey, Rayne)
Latin, meaning 'queen'.

Raissa
(alt. Raisa)
Yiddish, meaning 'rose'.

Raleigh
(alt. Rayleigh)
English, meaning 'meadow of roe deer'.

Rama
(alt. Ramey, Ramya)
Hebrew, meaning 'exalted'.

Ramona
(alt. Romona)
Spanish, meaning 'wise guardian'.

Ramsey
English, meaning 'raven island'.

Rana
(alt. Rania, Rayna)
Arabic, meaning 'beautiful thing'.

Randy
(alt. Randi)
Shortened form of Miranda, meaning 'admirable'.

Rani
Sanskrit, meaning 'queen'.

Raphaela
(alt. Rafaela, Raffaella)
Spanish, meaning 'healing God'.

Raquel
(alt. Racquel)
Hebrew, meaning 'ewe'.

Rashida
Turkish, meaning 'righteous'.

Raven
(alt. Ravyn)
English, from the bird of the same name.

Razia
Arabic, meaning 'contented'.

Reagan
(alt. Reagen, Regan)
Irish Gaelic, meaning 'descendant of Riagán'.

Reba
Shortened form of Rebecca, meaning 'joined'.

Rebecca
(alt. Rebekah)
Hebrew, meaning 'joined'.

Reese
Welsh, meaning 'fiery and zealous'.

Regina
Latin, meaning 'queen'.

Reiko
Japanese, meaning 'thankful one'.

Reina
(alt. Reyna, Rheyna)
Spanish, meaning 'queen'.

Rena
(alt. Reena)
Hebrew, meaning 'serene'.

Renata
Latin, meaning 'reborn'.

Rene
Greek, meaning 'peace'.

Renée
(alt. Renae)
French, meaning 'reborn'.

Renita
Latin, meaning 'resistant'.

Reshma
(alt. Resha)
Sanskrit, meaning 'silk'.

Reta
(alt. Retha, Retta)
Shortened form of Margaret, meaning 'pearl'.

Rhea
Greek, meaning 'earth'.

Rheta
Greek, meaning 'eloquent speaker'.

Rhiannon
(alt. Reanna, Reanne, Rhian, Rhianna)
Welsh, meaning 'witch'.

Rhoda
Greek, meaning 'rose'.

Rhona
Nordic, meaning 'rough island'.

Rhonda
(alt. Ronda)
Welsh, meaning 'noisy'.

Ría
(alt. Rie, Riya)
Shortened form of Victoria, meaning 'victor'.

Ricki
(alt. Rieko, Rika, Rikki)
Shortened form of Frederica, meaning 'peaceful ruler'.

Riley
Irish Gaelic, meaning 'courageous'.

Rilla
German, meaning 'small brook'.

Rima
Arabic, meaning 'antelope'.

Riona

Irish Gaelic, meaning 'like a queen'.

Ripley

English, meaning 'shouting man's meadow'.

Risa

Latin, meaning 'laughter'.

Rita

Shortened form of Margaret, meaning 'pearl'.

River
(alt. Riviera)

English, from the body of water of the same name.

Robbie
(alt. Robi, Roby)

Shortened form of Roberta, meaning 'bright fame'.

Roberta

English, meaning 'bright fame'.

Robin
(alt. Robbin, Robyn)

English, meaning 'bright fame'.

Rochelle
(alt. Richelle, Rochel)

French, meaning 'little rock'.

Rogue

French, meaning 'beggar'.

Rohina
(alt. Rohini)

Sanskrit, meaning 'sandalwood'.

Roisin

Irish Gaelic, meaning 'little rose'.

Roja

Spanish, meaning 'red-haired lady'.

Rolanda

German, meaning 'famous land'.

Roma

Italian, meaning 'Rome'.

Romaine
(alt. Romina)

French, meaning 'from Rome'.

'Powerful' names

Adira
Edrea
Isis
Ricarda
Roxie
Ulrika

Romola
(alt. Romilda, Romily)
Latin, meaning 'Roman woman'.

Romy
Shortened form of Rosemary, meaning 'dew of the sea'.

Rona
(alt. Ronia, Ronja, Ronna)
Nordic, meaning 'rough island'.

Ronnie
(alt. Roni)
English, meaning 'strong counsel'.

Roro
Indonesian, meaning 'nobility'.

Rosa
Italian, meaning 'rose'.

Rosabel
(alt. Rosabella)
Contraction of Rose and Belle, meaning 'beautiful rose'.

Rosalie
(alt. Rosale, Rosalia, Rosalina)
French, meaning 'rose garden'.

Rosalind
(alt. Rosalinda)
Spanish, meaning 'pretty rose'.

Rosalyn
(alt. Rosaleen, Rosaline, Roselyn)
Contraction of Rose and Lynn, meaning 'pretty rose'.

Rosamond
(alt. Rosamund)
German, meaning 'renowned protector'.

Rose
Latin, from the flower of the same name.

R

329

Roseanne
(alt. Rosana, Rosann, Rosanna, Rosanne, Roseann, Roseanna)

Contraction of Rose and Anne, meaning 'graceful rose'.

Rosemary
(alt. Rosemarie)

Latin, meaning 'dew of the sea'.

Rosie
(alt. Rosia)

Shortened form of Rosemary, meaning 'dew of the sea'.

Rosita

Spanish, meaning 'rose'.

Rowena
(alt. Rowan)

Welsh, meaning 'slender and fair'.

Roxanne
(alt. Roxana, Roxane, Roxanna)

Persian, meaning 'dawn'.

Roxie

Shortened form of Roxanne, meaning 'dawn'.

Rubena
(alt. Rubina)

Hebrew, meaning 'behold, a son'.

Ruby
(alt. Rubi, Rubie)

English, meaning 'red gemstone'.

Rusty

American, meaning 'red-headed'.

Ruth
(alt. Ruthe, Ruthie)

Hebrew, meaning 'friend and companion'.

Popular Irish names

Aoife
Aisling
Caitlin
Ciara
Eilis
Eimear
Niamh
Orlaith
Roisin
Saoirse

R

 Girls' names

Saba
(alt. Sabah)
Greek, meaning 'from Sheba'.

Sabina
(alt. Sabine)
Latin, meaning 'from the Sabine tribe'.

Sabrina
Latin, meaning 'the River Severn'.

Sadella
American, meaning 'fairytale princess'.

Sadie
(alt. Sade, Sadye)
Hebrew, meaning 'princess'.

Saffron
English, from the spice of the same name.

Safiya
Arabic, meaning 'sincere friend'.

Sage
(alt. Saga, Saige)
Latin, meaning 'wise and healthy'.

Sahara
Arabic, meaning 'desert'.

Sakura
Japanese, meaning 'cherry blossom'.

Sally
(alt. Sallie)
Hebrew, meaning 'princess'.

Salome
(alt. Salma)
Hebrew, meaning 'peace'.

Sam
(alt. Sammie, Sammy)
Shortened form of Samantha, meaning 'told by God'.

Samantha
Hebrew, meaning 'told by God'.

Samara
(alt. Samaria, Samira)
Hebrew, meaning 'under God's rule'.

Sanaa
Arabic, meaning 'brilliance'.

Sandra
(alt. Saundra)
Shortened form of Alexandra, meaning 'defender of mankind'.

Sandy
(alt. Sandi)
Shortened form of Sandra, meaning 'defender of mankind'.

Sangeeta
Hindi, meaning 'musical'.

Sanna
(alt. Saniya, Sanne, Sanni)
Hebrew, meaning 'lily'.

Santana
(alt. Santina)
Spanish, meaning 'holy'.

Saoirse
Irish, meaning 'freedom'.

Sapphire
(alt. Saphira)
Hebrew, meaning 'blue gemstone'.

Sarah
(alt. Sara, Sarai, Sariah)
Hebrew, meaning 'princess'.

Sasha
(alt. Sacha, Sascha)
Russian, meaning 'man's defender'.

Saskia
(alt. Saskie)
Dutch, meaning 'the Saxon people'.

Savannah
(alt. Savanah, Savanna, Savina)
Spanish, meaning 'treeless'.

Scarlett
(alt. Scarlet)
English, meaning 'scarlet'.

Scout
French, meaning 'to listen'.

Sedona
(alt. Sedna)
Spanish, from the city of the same name.

Selah
(alt Sela)
Hebrew, meaning 'cliff'.

Selby
English, meaning 'manor village'.

Selena
(alt. Salena, Salima, Salina, Selene, Selina)
Greek, meaning 'moon goddess'.

Selma
German, meaning 'Godly helmet'.

Seneca
Native American, meaning 'from the Seneca tribe'.

Sephora
Hebrew, meaning 'bird'.

September
Latin, meaning 'seventh month'.

Seraphina
(alt. Serafina, Seraphia, Seraphine)
Hebrew, meaning 'ardent'.

Serena
(alt. Sarina, Sereana)
Latin, meaning 'tranquil'.

Serenity
Latin, meaning 'serene'.

Shania
(alt. Shaina, Shana, Shaniya)
Hebrew, meaning 'beautiful'.

Shanice

American, meaning 'from Africa'.

Shaniqua
(alt. Shanika)

African, meaning 'warrior princess'.

Shanna

English, meaning 'old'.

Shannon
(alt. Shannan, Shanon)

Irish Gaelic, meaning 'old and ancient'.

Shantal
(alt. Shantel, Shantell)

French, meaning 'stone'.

Shanti

Hindi, meaning 'peaceful'.

Sharlene

German, meaning 'man'.

Sharon
(alt. Sharen, Sharona, Sharron, Sharyn)

Hebrew, meaning 'a plain'.

Nautical names

Coral
Genevieve
Halimedi
Marina
Nereida
Sagara

Shasta

American, from the mountain of the same name.

Shauna
(alt. Shawna)

Irish, meaning 'the Lord is gracious'.

Shayla
(alt. Shaylie, Shayna, Sheyla)

Irish, meaning 'blind'.

Shea

Irish Gaelic, meaning 'from the fairy fort'.

Sheena

Irish, meaning 'the Lord is gracious'.

Sheila
(alt. Shelia)
Irish, meaning 'blind'.

Shelby
(alt. Shelba, Shelbie)
English, meaning 'estate on the ledge'.

Shelley
(alt. Shelli, Shellie, Shelly)
English, meaning 'meadow on the ledge'.

Shenandoah
Native American, meaning 'after an Oneida chief'.

Sheridan
Irish Gaelic, meaning 'wild man'.

Sherry
(alt. Sheree, Sheri, Sherie, Sherri, Sherrie)
Shortened form of Cheryl, meaning 'man'.

Sheryl
(alt. Sherryl)
German, meaning 'man'.

Shiloh
Hebrew, meaning 'his gift'. From the biblical place of the same name.

Shirley
(alt. Shirlee)
English, meaning 'bright meadow'.

Shivani
Sanskrit, meaning 'wife of Shiva'.

Shona
Irish Gaelic, meaning 'God is gracious'.

Shoshana
(alt. Shoshanna)
Hebrew, meaning 'lily'.

Shura
Russian, meaning 'man's defender'.

Sian
(alt. Sianna)
Welsh, meaning 'the Lord is gracious'.

Sibyl
(alt. Sybil)
Greek, meaning 'seer and oracle'.

Sidney
(alt. Sydney)
English, meaning 'from St Denis'.

Sidonie
(alt. Sidonia, Sidony)
Latin, meaning 'from Sidonia'.

Siena
(alt. Sienna)
Latin, from the town of the same name.

Sierra
Spanish, meaning 'saw'.

Siffhi
Hindi, meaning 'spiritual powers'.

Signa
(alt. Signe)
Scandinavian, meaning 'victory'.

Sigrid
Nordic, meaning 'fair victory'.

Silja
Scandinavian, meaning 'blind'.

Simcha
Hebrew, meaning 'joy'.

Simone
(alt. Simona)
Hebrew, meaning 'listening intently'.

Sinead
Irish, meaning 'the Lord is gracious'.

Siobhan
Irish, meaning 'the Lord is gracious'.

Siren
(alt. Sirena)
Greek, meaning 'entangler'.

Siria
Spanish, meaning 'glowing'.

Sisika
Native American, meaning 'like a bird'.

Skye
(alt. Sky)
Scottish, from the island of the same name.

Skyler
(alt. Skyla, Skylar)
Dutch, meaning 'giving shelter'.

Sloane
(alt. Sloan)
Irish Gaelic, meaning 'man of arms'.

Socorro
Spanish, meaning 'to aid'.

Sojourner
English, meaning 'temporary stay'.

Solana
Spanish, meaning 'sunlight'.

Solange
French, meaning 'with dignity'.

Soledad
Spanish, meaning 'solitude'.

Soleil
French, meaning 'sun'.

Solveig
Scandinavian, meaning 'woman of the house'.

Sona
Arabic, meaning 'golden one'.

Sonia
(alt. Sonja, Sonya)
Greek, meaning 'wisdom'.

Sophia
(alt. Sofia, Sofie, Sophie)
Greek, meaning 'wisdom'.

Sophronia
Greek, meaning 'sensible'.

Soraya
Persian, meaning 'princess'.

Sorcha
Irish Gaelic, meaning 'bright and shining'.

Sorrel
English, from the herb of the same name.

Stacey
(alt. Stacie, Stacy)
Greek, meaning 'resurrection'.

Star
(alt. Starla, Starr)
English, meaning 'star'.

Stella
Latin, meaning 'star'.

Stephanie
(alt. Stefanie, Stephani,
Stephania, Stephany)
Greek, meaning 'crowned'.

Sue
(alt. Susie, Suzy)
Shortened form of Susan,
meaning 'lily'.

Sukey
(alt. Sukey, Sukie)
Shortened form of Susan,
meaning 'lily'.

Summer
English, from the season of the
same name.

Sunday
English, meaning 'the first day'.

Sunny
(alt. Sun)
English, meaning 'of a pleasant
temperament'.

Suri
Persian, meaning 'red rose'.

Surya
Hindi, from the god of the
same name.

Susan
(alt. Susann, Suzan)
Hebrew, meaning 'lily'.

Susannah
(alt. Susana, Susanna, Susanne,
Suzanna, Suzanne)
Hebrew, meaning 'lily'.

Svea
Swedish, meaning 'of the
motherland'.

Svetlana
Russian, meaning 'star'.

Swanhild
Saxon, meaning 'battle swan'.

Sylvia
(alt. Silvia, Sylvie)
Latin, meaning 'from the
forest'.

T Girls' names

Tabitha
(alt. Tabatha)
Aramaic, meaning 'gazelle'.

Tahira
Arabic, meaning 'virginal'.

Tai
Chinese, meaning 'big'.

Taima
(alt. Taina)
Native American, meaning 'peal of thunder'.

Tajsa
Polish, meaning 'princess'.

Talia
(alt. Tali)
Hebrew, meaning 'heaven's dew'.

Taliesin
Welsh, meaning 'shining brow'.

Talise
(alt. Talyse)
Native American, meaning 'lovely water'.

Talitha
Aramaic, meaning 'young girl'.

Tallulah
(alt. Taliyah)
Native American, meaning 'leaping water'.

Tamara
(alt. Tamera)
Hebrew, meaning 'palm tree'.

Tamatha
(alt. Tametha)
American, meaning 'dear Tammy'.

Tamera
Hebrew, meaning 'palm tree'.

Tamika
(alt. Tameka)
American, meaning 'people'.

Tammy
(alt. Tami, Tammie)
Shortened form of Tamsin, meaning 'twin'.

Tamsin
Hebrew, meaning 'twin'.

Tanis
Spanish, meaning 'to make famous'.

Tanya
(alt. Tania, Tanya, Tonya)
Shortened form of Tatiana, meaning 'from the Tatius clan'.

Tao
Chinese, meaning 'like a peach'.

Tara
(alt. Tahra, Tarah, Tera)
Irish Gaelic, meaning 'rocky hill'.

Tasha
(alt. Taisha, Tarsha)
Shortened form of Natasha, meaning 'Christmas'.

Tatiana
(alt. Tayana)
Russian, meaning 'from the Tatius clan'.

Tatum
English, meaning 'light hearted'.

Tawny
(alt. Tawanaa, Tawnee, Tawnya)
English, meaning 'golden brown'.

Taya
Greek, meaning 'poor one'.

Taylor
(alt. Tayler)
English, meaning 'tailor'.

Tea
Greek, meaning 'goddess'.

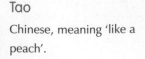

Teagan
(alt. Teague, Tegan)
Irish Gaelic, meaning 'poet'.

Teal
English, from the bird of the same name.

Tecla
Greek, meaning 'fame of God'.

Tehile
Hebrew, meaning 'song of praise'.

Temperance
English, meaning 'virtue'.

Tempest
French, meaning 'storm'.

Teresa
(alt. Terese, Tereza, Theresa, Therese)
Greek, meaning 'harvest'.

Terry
(alt. Teri, Terrie)
Shortened form of Teresa, meaning 'harvest'.

Tessa
(alt. Tess, Tessie)
Shortened form of Teresa, meaning 'harvest'.

Thais
Greek, from the mythological heroine of the same name.

Thalia
Greek, meaning 'blooming'.

Thandi
(alt. Thana)
Arabic, meaning 'thanksgiving'.

Thea
Greek, meaning 'goddess'.

Theda
German, meaning 'people'.

Thelma
Greek, meaning 'will'.

Theodora
Greek, meaning 'gift of God'.

Theodosia
Greek, meaning 'gift of God'.

Thisbe

Greek, from the mythological heroine of the same name.

Thomasina

(alt. Thomasin, Thomasine, Thomasyn)

Greek, meaning 'twin'.

Thora

Scandinavian, meaning 'Thor's struggle'.

Tia

(alt. Tiana)

Spanish, meaning 'aunt'.

Tiara

Latin, meaning 'jewelled headband'.

Tien

Vietnamese, meaning 'fairy child'.

Tierney

Irish Gaelic, meaning 'Lord'.

Tierra

(alt. Tiera)

Spanish, meaning 'land'.

Tiffany

(alt. Tiffani, Tiffanie)

Greek, meaning 'God's appearance'.

Tiggy

Shortened form of Tigris, meaning 'tiger'.

Tigris

Irish Gaelic, meaning 'tiger'.

Tilda

Shortened form of Matilda, meaning 'battle-mighty'.

Tillie

(alt. Tilly)

Shortened form of Matilda, meaning 'battle-mighty'.

Timothea

Greek, meaning 'honouring God'.

Tina

(alt. Teena, Tena)

Shortened form of Christina, meaning 'anointed Christian'.

Tirion

Welsh, meaning 'kind and gentle'.

T

Tirzah

Hebrew, meaning 'pleasantness'.

Titania

Greek, meaning 'giant'.

Toby

(alt. Tobi)

Hebrew, meaning 'God is good'.

Tomoko

Japanese, meaning 'intelligent'.

Toni

(alt. Tony)

Latin, meaning 'invaluable'.

Tonia

(alt. Tonja, Tonya)

Russian, meaning 'praiseworthy'.

Topaz

Latin, meaning 'golden gemstone'.

Tori

(alt. Tora)

Shortened form of Victoria, meaning 'victory'.

Tova

(alt. Tovah, Tove)

Hebrew, meaning 'good'.

Tracy

(alt. Tracey, Tracie)

Greek, meaning 'harvest'.

Treva

Welsh, meaning 'homestead'.

Tricia

Shortened form of Patricia, meaning 'aristocratic'.

Trilby

English, meaning 'vocal trills'. Also a kind of hat.

Trina

(alt. Trena)

Greek, meaning 'pure'.

Autumn names

Aeria
Axelle
Peace
Shanti
Zulma

Trinity

Latin, meaning 'triad'.

Trisha

Shortened form of Patricia, meaning 'noble'.

Trista

Latin, meaning 'sad'.

Trixie

Shortened form of Beatrix, meaning 'bringer of gladness'.

Trudy

(alt. Tru, Trudie)

Shortened form of Gertrude, meaning 'strength of a spear'.

Tullia

Spanish, meaning 'bound for glory'.

Tunder

Hungarian, meaning 'fairy'.

Twyla

(alt. Twila)

American, meaning 'star'.

Tyler

English, meaning 'tiler'.

Tyra

Scandinavian, meaning 'Thor's struggle'.

Tzipporah

Hebrew, meaning 'bird'.

Popular Scottish names

Alana
Catriona
Elsie
Elspeth
Flora
Heather
Isla
Kirsty
Morag
Rhona

T

 Girls' names

Udaya
Indian, meaning 'dawn'.

Ula
(alt. Ulla)
Celtic, meaning 'gem of the sea'.

Ulrika
(alt. Urica)
German, meaning 'power of the wolf'.

Uma
Sanskrit, meaning 'flax'.

Una
Latin, meaning 'one'.

Undine
Latin, meaning 'little wave'.

> **Famous athletes**
>
> Denise (Lewis)
> Jessica (Ennis)
> Kelly (Holmes)
> Mary (Rand)
> Paula (Radcliffe)
> Sally (Gunnell)
> Sarah (Storey)
>
>

Unice
Greek, meaning 'victorious'.

Unique
Latin, meaning 'only one'.

Unity
English, meaning 'oneness'.

U

Uriela

Hebrew, meaning 'God's light'.

Urja
(alt. Urjitha)

Indian, meaning 'energy'.

Ursula

Latin, meaning 'little female bear'.

Uta

German, meaning 'prospers in battle'.

Popular South American names

Adriel	Frances
Albany	Lily
Carolina	Mariana
Elena	Natalia
Eréndira	Poppy

U

Girls' names

Vada

German, meaning 'famous ruler'.

Valdis

(alt. Valdiss, Valdys, Valdyss)

Norse, meaning 'goddess of the dead', based on the mythological goddess of the same name.

Vale

Shortened form of Valencia, meaning 'strong and healthy'.

Valencia

(alt. Valancy, Valarece)

Latin, meaning 'strong and healthy'.

Valentina

Latin, meaning 'strong and healthy'.

Valentine

Latin, from the saint of the same name.

Valeria

Latin, meaning 'to be healthy and strong'.

Valerie

(alt. Valarie, Valery, Valorie)

Latin, meaning 'to be healthy and strong'.

Valia
(alt. Vallie)

Shortened form of Valerie, meaning 'to be healthy and strong'.

Vandana

Sanskrit, meaning 'worship'.

Vanessa
(alt. Vanesa)

English, from the *Gulliver's Travels* character of the same name.

Vanetta
(alt. Vanettah, Vaneta, Vanete, Vanity)

Greek, alternative of Vanessa, meaning 'like a butterfly'.

Vanity

Latin, meaning 'self-obsessed'.

Vashti

Persian, meaning 'beauty'.

Veda

Sanskrit, meaning 'knowledge and wisdom'.

Vega

Arabic, meaning 'falling vulture'.

Velda

German, meaning 'ruler'.

Vella

American, meaning 'beautiful'.

Velma

English, meaning 'determined protector'.

Venice
(alt. Venetia, Venita)

Latin, meaning 'city of canals'. From the city of the same name.

Venus

Latin, from the Roman goddess of the same name.

Vera
(alt. Verla, Verlie)

Slavic, meaning 'faith'.

Verda
(alt. Verdie)

Latin, meaning 'spring-like'.

Christmas names

Angel
Holly
Ivy
Mary
Natalie
Robyn

Verena

Latin, meaning 'true'.

Verity

Latin, meaning 'truth'.

Verna
(alt. Vernie)

Latin, meaning 'spring green'.

Verona

Latin, shortened form of Veronica. From the city of the same name.

Veronica
(alt. Verica, Veronique)

Latin, meaning 'true image'.

Veruca

Latin, meaning 'wart'.

Vesta

Latin, from the Roman goddess of the same name.

Vevina

Scottish, meaning 'pleasant lady'.

Vicenta

Latin, meaning 'prevailing'.

Vicky
(alt. Vicki, Vickie, Vikki, Vix)

Shortened form of Victoria, meaning 'victory'.

Victoria

Latin, meaning 'victory'.

Vida

Spanish, meaning 'life'.

Vidya

Sanskrit, meaning 'knowledge'.

Vienna

Latin, from the city of the same name.

Vigdis

Scandinavian, meaning 'war goddess'.

Vina
(alt. Vena)
Spanish, meaning 'vineyard'.

Viola
Latin, meaning 'violet'.

Violet
(alt. Violetta)
Latin, meaning 'purple'.

Virgie
Shortened form of Virginia, meaning 'maiden'.

Virginia
(alt. Virginie)
Latin, meaning 'maiden'.

Visara
Sanskrit, meaning 'celestial'.

Vita
Latin, meaning 'life'.

Vittoria
Variation of Victoria, meaning 'victory'.

Viva
Latin, meaning 'alive'.

Viveca
Scandinavian, meaning 'war fortress'.

Vivian
(alt. Vivien, Vivienne)
Latin, meaning 'lively'.

Vonda
Czech, meaning 'from the tribe of Vandals'.

Food and drinks-inspired names

Anise
Brandy
Cinnamon
Coco
Ginger
Madeleine
Olive
Polenta
Saffron

V

Girls' names

Waleska
Polish, meaning 'beautiful'.

Wallis
English, meaning 'from Wales'.

Walta
African, meaning 'like a shield'.

Wanda
(alt. Waneta, Wanita)
Slavic, meaning 'tribe of the vandals'.

Waneta
(alt. Wanita)
Variation of Wanda, meaning 'tribe of the vandals'.

Wanita
Variation of Wanda meaning 'tribe of the vandals'.

Wava
English, meaning 'way'.

Waverly
Old English, meaning 'meadow of aspens'.

Wendy
English, meaning 'friend'.

Wharton
English, meaning 'from the river'.

Whisper
English, meaning 'whisper'.

Whitley
Old English, meaning 'white meadow'.

Whitney

Old English, meaning 'white island'.

Wilda

German, meaning 'willow tree'.

Wilfreda

English, feminine form of Wilfred, meaning 'to will peace'.

Wilhelmina

German, meaning 'determined'.

Willene

(alt. Willia, Willa)

German, meaning 'helmet'.

Willow

English, from the tree of the same name.

Wilma

German, meaning 'protection'.

Winifred

Old English, meaning 'holy and blessed'.

Winnie

Shortened form of Winifred, meaning 'holy and blessed'.

Winona

(alt. Wynona)

Indian, meaning 'first-born daughter'.

Winslow

English, meaning 'friend's hill'.

Winter

English, meaning 'winter'.

Wisteria

English, meaning 'flower'.

Wren

English, from the bird of the same name.

Wynda

Scottish, meaning 'of the narrow passage'.

Wynne

Welsh, meaning 'white'.

Bird names

Avis
Evelyn
Raven
Starling
Teal
Wren

352

 Girls' names

Xanadu
African, meaning 'of exotic
paradise'.

Xanthe
Greek, meaning 'blonde'.

Xanthippe
Greek, meaning 'nagging'.

Xaverie
Greek, meaning 'bright'.

Xaviera
Arabic, meaning 'bright'.

Xena
Greek, meaning 'foreigner'.

Xenia
Greek, meaning 'foreigner'.

Ximena
Greek, meaning 'listening'.

Xiomara
Spanish, meaning 'battle-
ready'.

Xiu
Chinese, meaning 'elegant'.

Xochitl
Spanish, meaning 'flower'.

Xoey
Variant of Zoe, meaning 'life'.

Xristina

Variation of Christina, meaning 'follower of Christ'.

Xylia

(alt. Xylina, Xyloma)

Greek, meaning 'from the woods'.

Popular Welsh names

Bronwen	Myfanwy
Carys/Cerys	Rhiannon
Elen	Sian
Guinevere	Tegan
Megan	Wynne

 Girls' names

Yadira
Arabic, meaning 'worthy'.

Yael
Hebrew, meaning 'mountain goat'.

Yaffa
(alt. Yahaira, Yajaira)
Hebrew, meaning 'lovely'.

Yamilet
Arabic, meaning 'beautiful'.

Yana
Hebrew, meaning 'the Lord is gracious'.

Yanha
Arabic, meaning 'dove-like'.

Yanira
Hawaiian, meaning 'pretty'.

Yareli
Latin, meaning 'golden'.

Yaretzi
(alt. Yaritza)
Hawaiian, meaning 'forever beloved'.

Yasmin
(alt. Yasmeen, Yasmina)
Persian, meaning 'jasmine flower'.

Yelena
Greek, meaning 'bright and chosen'.

Yeraldina
Spanish, meaning 'ruled with a spear'.

Yesenia
Arabic, meaning 'flower'.

Yetta

English, from Henrietta, meaning 'ruler of the house'.

Yeva

Hebrew variant of Eve, meaning 'life'.

Ylva

Old Norse, meaning 'sea wolf'.

Yoki
(alt. Yoko)

Native American, meaning 'rain'.

Yolanda
(alt. Yolonda)

Spanish, meaning 'violet flower'.

Yoselin

English, meaning 'lovely'.

Yoshiko

Japanese, meaning 'good child'.

Yovela

Hebrew, meaning 'jubilee'.

Ysabel

English, meaning 'God's promise'.

Fiery names

Ardea
Blaise
Enya
Nuri
Vesta

Ysanne

Contraction of Isabel and Anne, meaning 'pledged to God' and 'grace'.

Yuki

Japanese, meaning 'lucky'.

Yuliana

Latin, meaning 'youthful'.

Yuridia

Russian, meaning 'farmer'.

Yusia

Arabic, meaning 'success'.

Yvette
(alt. Yvonne)

French, meaning 'yew'.

Y

Z Girls' names

Zafira
Arabic, meaning 'successful'.

Zahara
(alt. Zahava, Zahra, Zayah)
Arabic, meaning 'flowering and shining'.

Zaida
(alt. Zaide)
Arabic, meaning 'prosperous'.

Zalika
Swahili, meaning 'well born'.

Zaltana
Arabic, meaning 'high mountain'.

Zamia
Greek, meaning 'pine cone'.

Zaneta
(alt. Zanceta, Zanetah, Zanett, Zanetta)
Hebrew, meaning 'a gracious present from God'.

Zaniyah
Arabic, meaning 'lily'.

Zara
(alt. Zaria, Zariah, Zora)
Arabic, meaning 'radiance'.

Zelda
German, meaning 'dark battle'.

Zelia
(alt. Zella)
Scandinavian, meaning 'sunshine'.

Zelma
German, meaning 'helmet'.

Zemirah
Hebrew, meaning 'joyous melody'.

Zena
(alt. Zenia, Zina)
Greek, meaning 'hospitable'.

Zenaida
Greek, meaning 'the life of Zeus'.

Zenobia
Latin, meaning 'the life of Zeus'.

Zephyr
Greek, meaning 'the west wind'.

Zetta
Italian, meaning 'Z'.

Zia
Arabic, meaning 'light and splendour'.

Zinaida
Greek, meaning 'belonging to Zeus'.

Zinnia
Latin, meaning 'flower'.

Zipporah
Hebrew, meaning 'bird'.

Zita
(alt. Ziva)
Spanish, meaning 'little girl'.

Zoe
(alt. Zoi, Zoie, Zoey, Zoeya)
Greek, meaning 'life'.

Zoila
Greek, meaning 'life'.

Zoraida
Spanish, meaning 'captivating woman'.

Zorina
Slavic, meaning 'golden'.

Zosia
(alt. Zosima)
Greek, meaning 'wisdom'.

Zoya
Greek, meaning 'life'.

Zula
African, meaning 'brilliant'.

Zuleika
Arabic, meaning 'fair and intelligent'.

Zulma
Arabic, meaning 'peace'.

Zuzana
Hebrew, meaning 'lily'.

Zuzu
Czech, meaning 'flower'.

Popular Australian names

Amelia
Charlotte
Chloe
Ella
Emily
Isabella
Mia
Olivia
Sienna
Sophie

Z

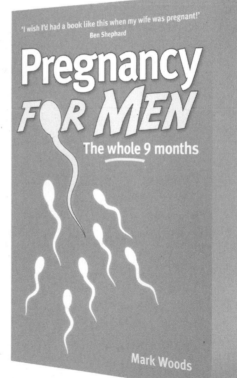